CW00556153

BEER

Norman Lambert & Ted Gosling

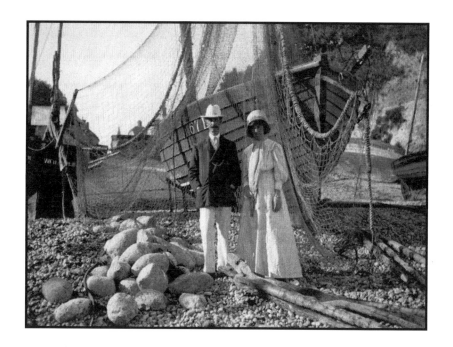

The
History
Press

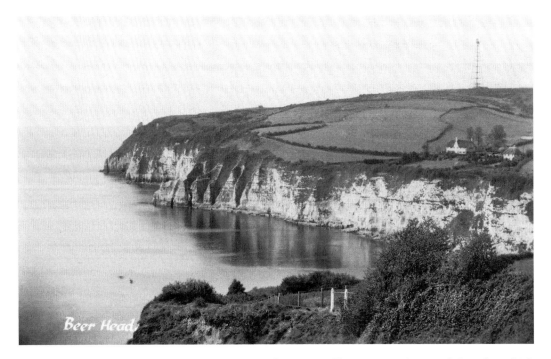

This splendid view from the cliff path looking towards Beer Head has a rare inclusion of the pylon which was erected during the Second World War to detect enemy aircraft.

Title page photograph: Holidaymakers posing beside a Beer trawler in 1905. Notice the ballast and fine nets.

Opposite: A peep through King's Isle Rock which is now filled with concrete.

First published 2011

The History Press
The Mill, Brimscombe Port
Stroud, Gloucestershire, GL5 2QG
www.thehistorypress.co.uk

© Norman Lambert and Ted Gosling, 2011

The right of Norman Lambert and Ted Gosling to be identified as
the Authors of this work has been asserted in accordance with
the Copyrights, Designs and Patents Act 1988.

British Library Cataloguing in Publication Data.
A catalogue record for this book is available from the British
Library.

ISBN 978 0 7524 6190 8

Typesetting and origination by The History Press
Printed in Great Britain

CONTENTS

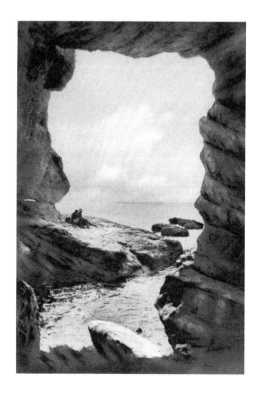

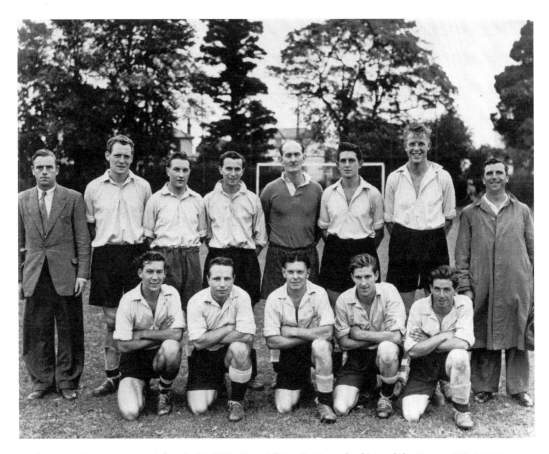

At the time this picture was taken in 1955/6, Beer Albion 1st team had joined the Exeter & District League and were a premier league side, having won the Senior 1 Championship the season before. This picture was taken at St Luke's College, Exeter. Back row, left to right: Maurice Webber (secretary and manager), Eddie Bond, Tony White, Lewis Perkins, Jimmy Jones, Ron Wilkins, Bob Aplin, 'Taffy' Fowler (trainer). Front row: Brian Northcott, Robbie Driver, Basil Agland, Arthur Critchard, Alan Westlake.

INTRODUCTION

In my days at Beer Church of England School, talk of past happenings and village history was a cruel strain on a young memory. Years afterwards I realised that such knowledge is an inheritance from which there is no escape, since history is something which explains the past in the present and points inevitably to the future.

In those school days it was simply a matter of learning names and dates. How interesting that has proved to be over the past six decades. An interest which has lasted and continues to this day.

In the book *The Village of Beer*, published in December 1999, the preface highlighted the colourful history of the village and stated there would be more to add following that publication. This further book on Beer is a pictorial illustration of years past and more modern records of village life as we move into the second decade of the twenty-first century. There will doubtless be the odd mistake and name missing, for which I apologise, but in the main the preparation has resulted from my extensive personal collection of original photographs and old postcards of the village accumulated over the years.

Ted Gosling, who started his working life in Beer back in the 1940s at Oborns Garage, has been the curator of the Axe Valley Museum since its inception in 1986. While Ted is a 'Seaton Boy', he feels he has served a sufficiently long and affectionate link with Beer to qualify as a near-local. I thank him for his invaluable assistance in the layout and preparation of this book, which both he and I trust will be of great interest to locals and visitors alike.

I am most proud to have been born in the village in 1937 and to have grown up among so many of the people who appear on the following pages, and in such lovely surroundings. While he is long gone, the feeling that without the strict discipline of Mr W.R. David (affectionately known as Pop), the headmaster of the school for thirty years (from 1918 to 1948), the village boys and girls might not have matured to the degree they have and accordingly I dedicate this book to his memory.

N.L.G. Lambert, April 2011

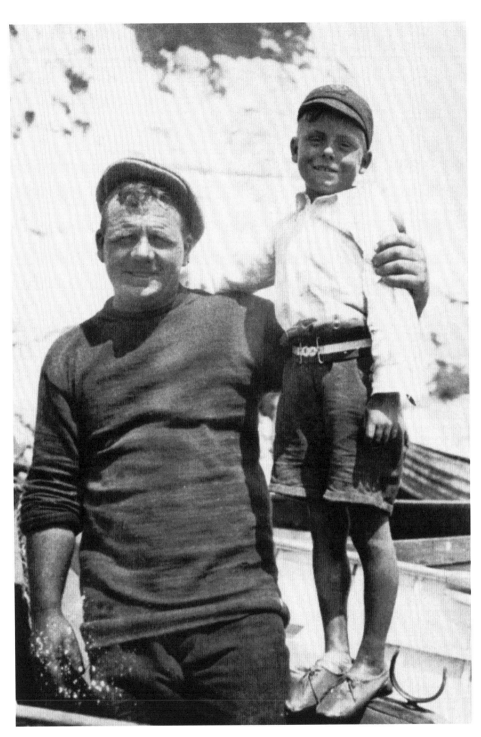

A young Rupert Aplin with his father (known as John Bull). The two generations ran a tea hut, beach huts, deck chair rentals and a mackerel fishing boat on Beer beach for more than fifty years.

1

FISHERMEN
OF BEER

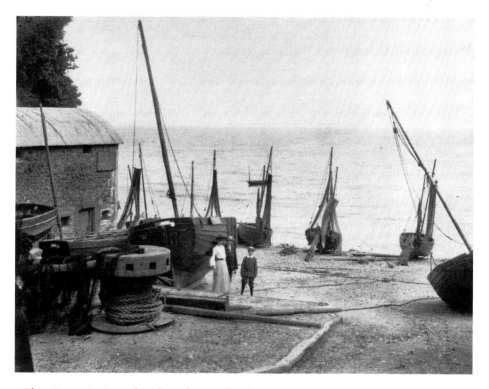

There is a majestic quality about this Beer beach scene which raises it far above the average.
The Edwardian style of clothes might help to guess an approximate date.

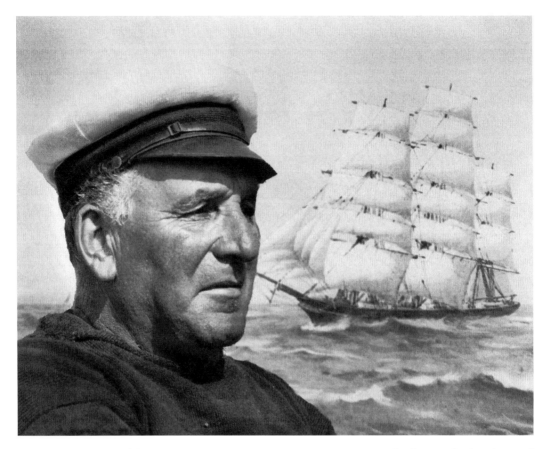

Charles Chapple, Beer fisherman, *c.* 1948. Born in Beer on 4 January 1876, Charles was the fourth son of James Chapple, a fisherman of Beer. Charles Chapple, like all Beer boys, was born for the sea and started fishing at the age of twelve as 'the boy' in a local trawler. When he was nineteen he joined the Royal Navy and trained as a stoker. He was rated Stoker Petty Officer on 7 April 1906 and retired from the Royal Navy with the rank of Stoker Chief Petty Officer in 1919. While in the RN he was landed in the Naval Brigade and was a fireman on one of the railway steam engines that hauled the heavy naval guns to 'Spion Kop', which earned him a special recommendation. Later he saw action in the Battle of Jutland and more war service in the new torpedo boats; finally he qualified in the use of oil-fired boilers. On his retirement to Beer he operated and owned an 18ft motor boat, the *Kathleen*, taking fishing trips in the bay. He was a well-known and colourful personality, who died in the late 1950s.

Opposite: These magnificent old photographs, taken by a visitor in 1890, show how busy it was when the boats returned with their daily catch. Note the horse and cart as the transport, and the tubs where the fish was loaded for forwarding by train from Seaton to Billingsgate Market in London.

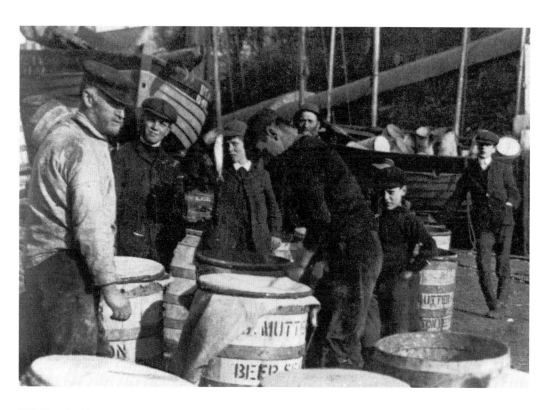

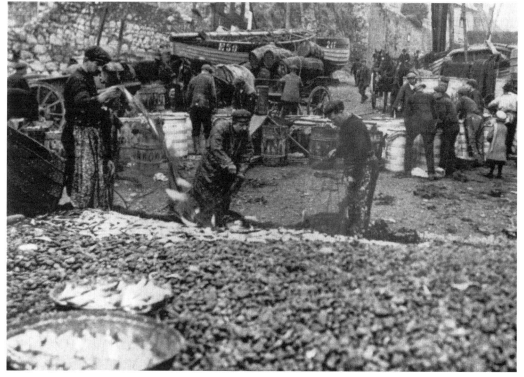

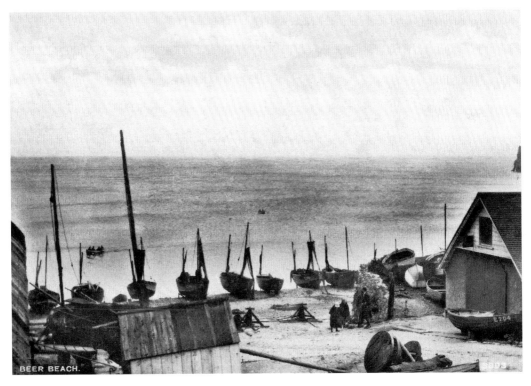

A 1930s view of the beach and boats with Charlie's Yard and Reg Hurley's workshop.

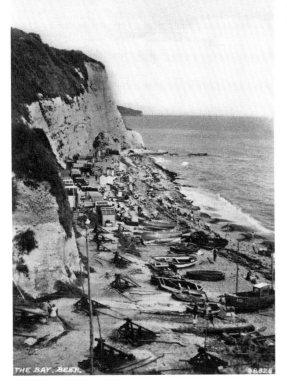

Beer beach with boats, beach huts and many holidaymakers in the early 1950s.

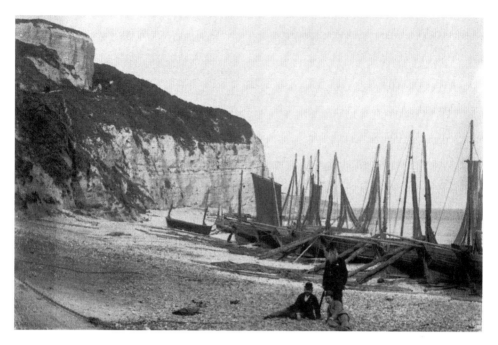

Part of the Beer fleet at rest. Note the cliff, where the path down to the beach had not yet been formed – so this photo dates back to before 1878.

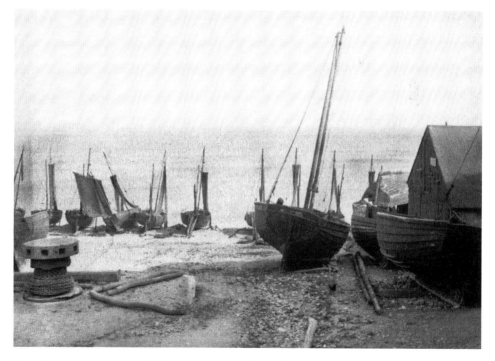

The big capstan and some fishing boats at rest. The building on the right is Charlie's Yard which was a maintenance shop.

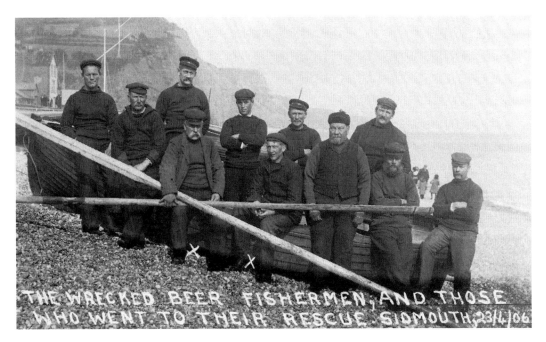

The caption on the postcard tells it all – 23 April 1906.

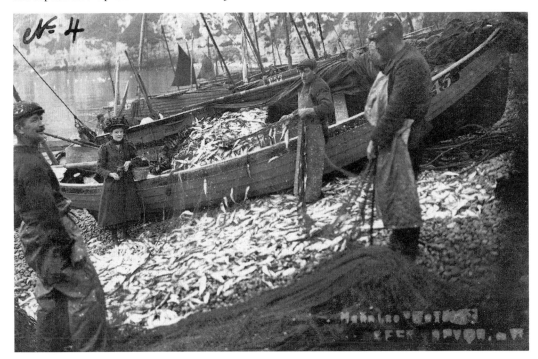

A fantastic catch of herring, 300,000 in one day in 1925. The person in the centre is Albert Bartlett. Sadly much of this catch was allowed to rot or was used for manure on the allotments above, since the carriage for sending a barrel was 8s and the sale price at Billingsgate only 7s 6d. So after the inhabitants had taken what they wanted – the remainder went to waste.

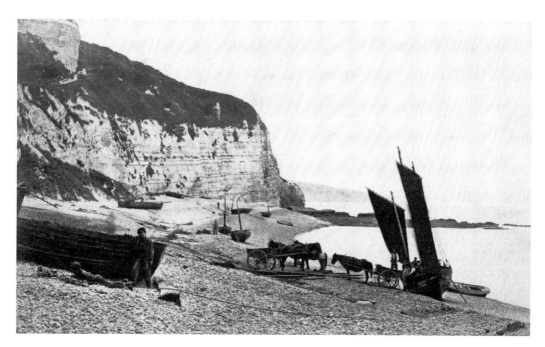

Another early picture, before 1878, showing the transport of the time. The carts were ready to haul the catch up the beach and subsequently Sea Hill.

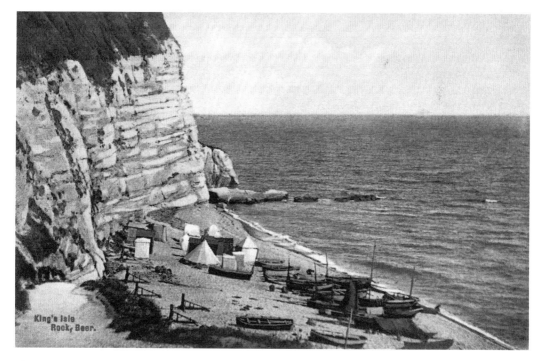

This picture postcard, posted in July 1911 from Beer, shows the early bathing booths, capstans and boats on the eastern side of Beer beach, with King's Isle Rock being prevalent.

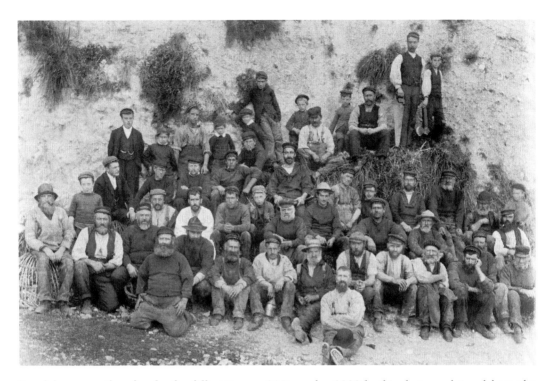

Beer fishermen gathered under the cliffs at Beer on 31 December 1899 for this photograph to celebrate the turn of the century.

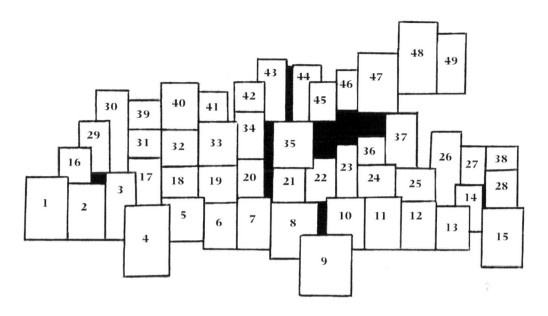

Key to photograph of Beer fishermen (opposite)

1	Ned Marshall (Sailmaker)	26	Bob Gibbs
2	Jacob Blackmore	27	Jack Ayres
3	Bill Marshall	28	Dan Perry
4	Tom Russell (drowned in trawler)	29	Frank Thorn
5	Tom Woodgate	30	Jim Leyman
6	Jack Russell	31	Will Mutter
7	Billy Agland	32	Harry Bartlett
8	Jim Bartlett	33	William R. Driver
9	Billy Roe	34	Ernest Miller
10	Bobby Driver	35	Mr Bending (Coastguard)
11	Jack Newton	36	Norman Miller
12	Bill Russell	37	Mr Triggs (Coastguard)
13	Theodore Boalch	38	-?-
14	Dick Ayres (drowned in trawler)	39	Willie Horner
15	Bill Miller (drowned in trawler)	40	Jethroe Westlake
16	Albert Ayres	41	-?-
17	Will Chapple	42	-?-
18	Coastguard	43	Joe Russell
19	Ben Potter	44	Tommy Westlake
20	Albert Roe	45	Joe Miller
21	Billy Woodgate	46	-?-
22	Bill Orley	47	Fred Driver
23	-?-	48	Tom Restorick (Boatbuilder)
24	George Edwards	49	Will Restorick (Apprentice)
25	Tom White		

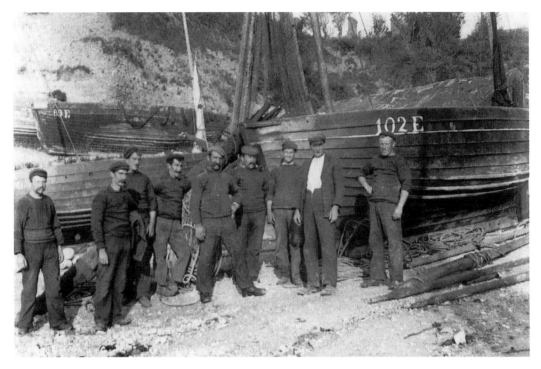

'On the Land' – a collection of Beer fishermen at about the turn of the last century or perhaps in the 1890s.

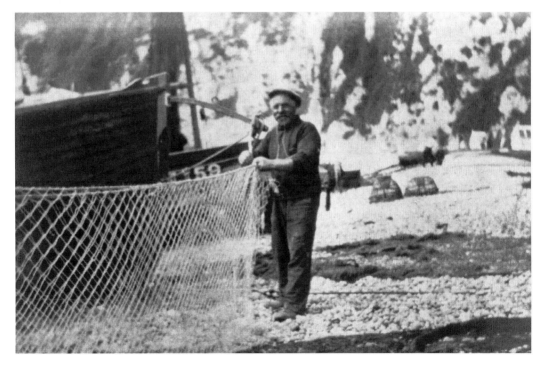

An 'old salt' mending his nets – note the crab pots in the background.

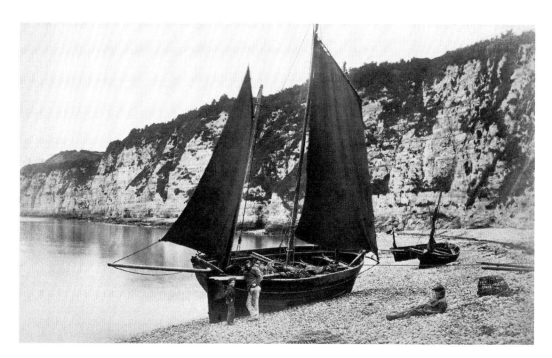

A three-masted fishing lugger on Beer beach,
August 1877. The Beer fishing fleet boat,
a clinker-built craft, was ideal for the job.
Constructed of elm or oak frames, the boats
were built in the village with sailing qualities
known far and wide. The sails of these boats
were made by the fishermen and their families
and barked with Burma Cutch to preserve the
canvas. In this photograph, the three-mast Beer
lugger beached broadside on with full tackle
on board is waiting to go to sea. The sheltered
position of the beach allowed fishermen from
Beer to put to sea, when others from Seaton and
Sidmouth were weatherbound, giving them a
reputation of unsurpassed seamanship.

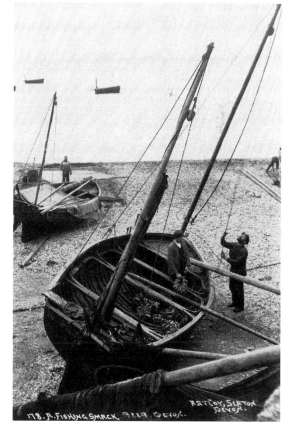

A fine picture of a Beer fishing smack – there
was no engine at the time of this postcard which
was postmarked Beer in 1908.

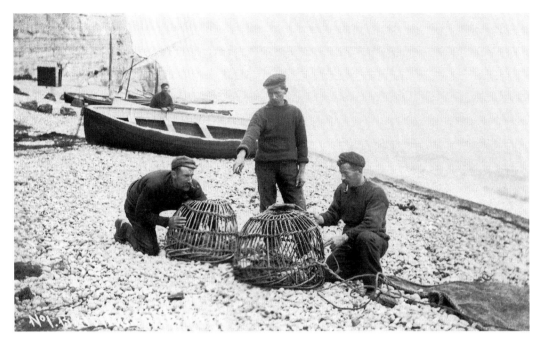

This picture shows three Beer fishermen either baiting or unloading the crab pots which they probably would have made themselves, *c.* 1900.

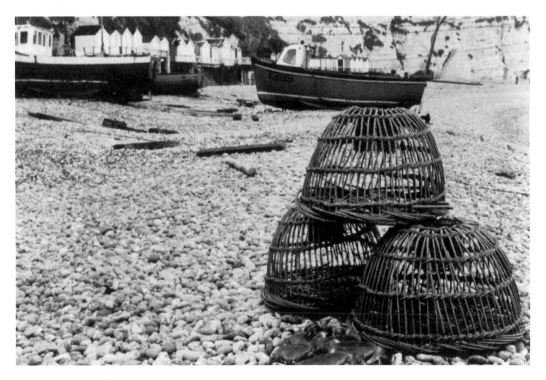

Just returned with the crabs beside the pots which trapped them.

'Chunky' Bartlett making a crab pot – he is the last of the Beer fishermen to have the art, which in the past so many held.

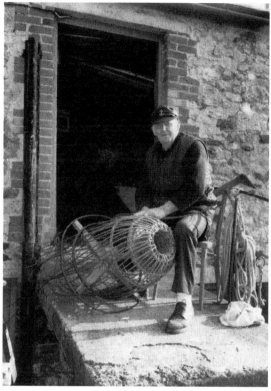

Another fine photograph of Beer beach looking east, *c.* 1900.

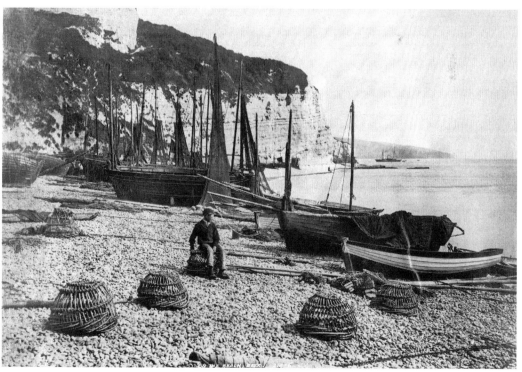

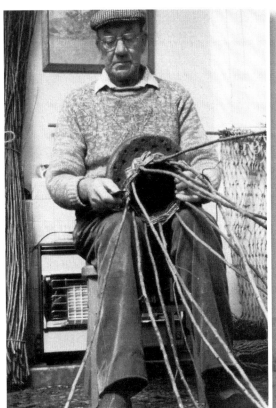

Fred Newton making crab pots, 1982.

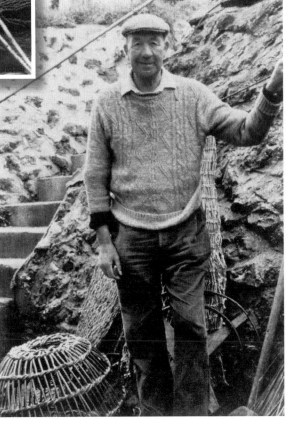

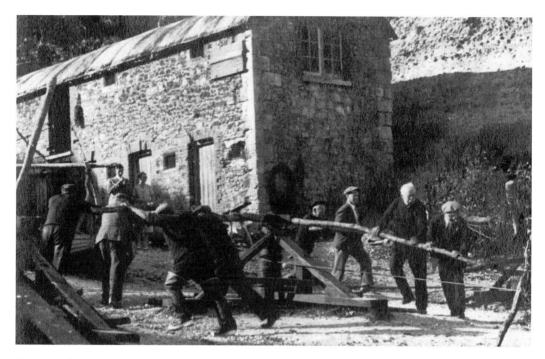

Men at work! Hauling up a boat around the capstan, *c.* 1930.

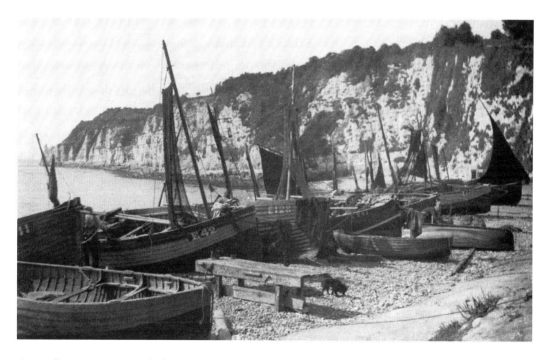

A very illustrative picture of a busy fishing village with the beach full of boats, all under sail, *c.* 1910. It was a hard life for those who manned them. The local fishing industry was at its peak and the seamanship of the Beer men was well-known and respected.

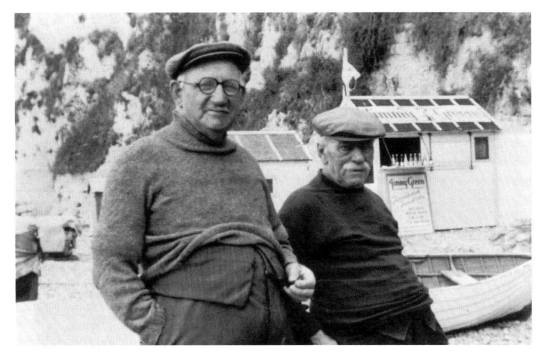

Above: Two life-long mates on Beer beach in 1951: Jim Westlake and Joe Bartlett – what tales they had to tell!

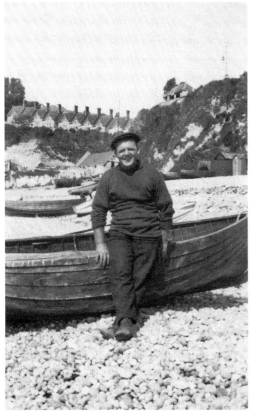

Left: This picture shows a young Norman Aplin (John Bull), later famous for his tea hut. The fishermen's cottages are in the background.

Opposite: An early picture of two of the tea huts on the beach, namely those of Aplin and Driver, *c.* 1930. Tea was 2*d* a cup.

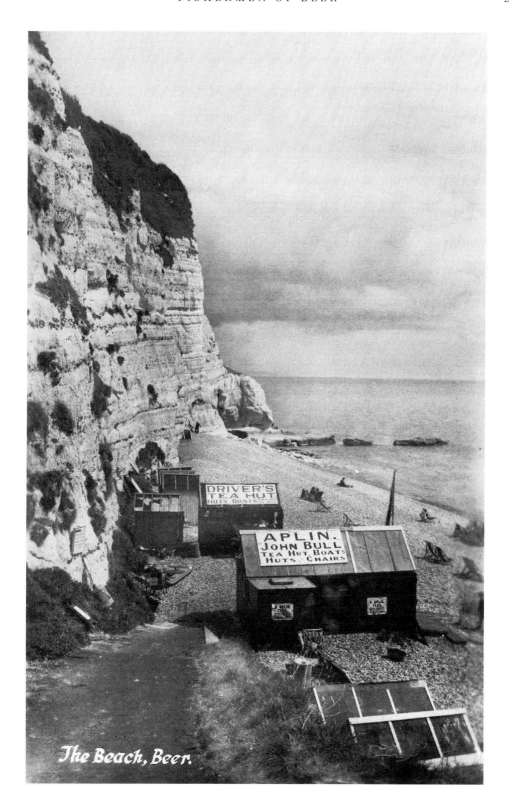

The Beach, Beer.

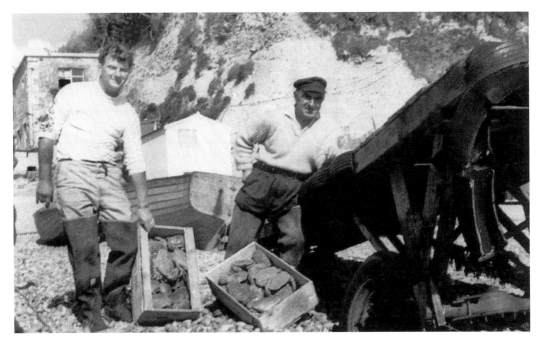

John Wakley ('Whiskey') and Les Paddy with two boxes of crabs, *c.* 1960.

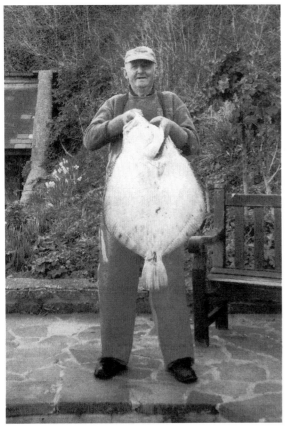

Peter Bartlett ('Chunky') with a very large 56lb turbot which he caught in 1998.

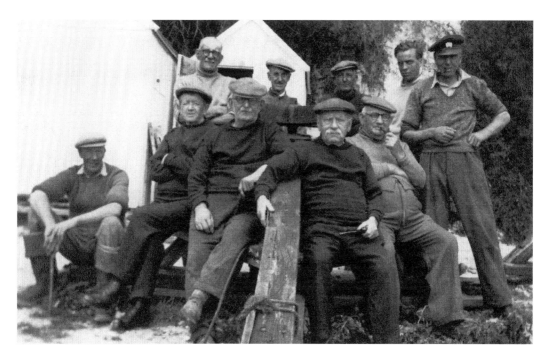

A group of Beer fishermen in about 1958. Front row, left to right: Fred Newton, Garnet Miller, 'Waddy' Woodgate, Joe Bartlett, Jim Westlake. Back row: Bert Bond, Tom Russell, Jack Westlake, Roy Newton, Dougie Orley.

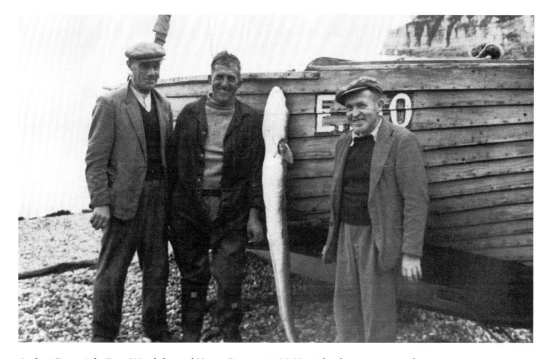

Arthur Restorick, Tom Westlake and Harry Barrett in 1948 with a large conger eel.

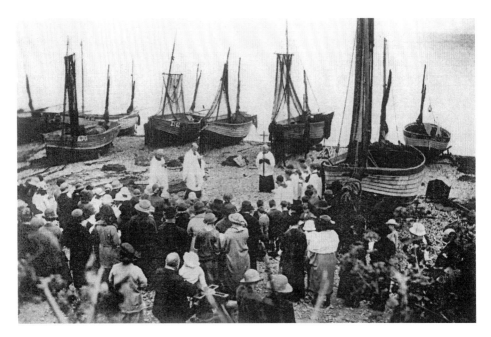

Rogation Sunday service on Beer beach, 1926.

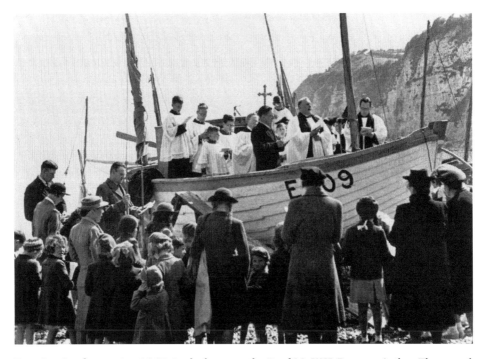

Rogation Sunday service, 1948. In the boat are the Revd Mr W.H. Dormer, Arthur Thorn and Mr Billingsley (organist). On the beach are Les Miller, Daphne Ham, Fred Hoskins and Mrs Dormer. The boy in the boat , third on the left, is Norman Lambert and the one in the middle Richard Cullen.

William Rattenbury Esq. was the last of the smugglers. These photographs, one dating from 1865 and the other from 1871, illustrate the only known pictures of Jack Rattenbury's oldest son.

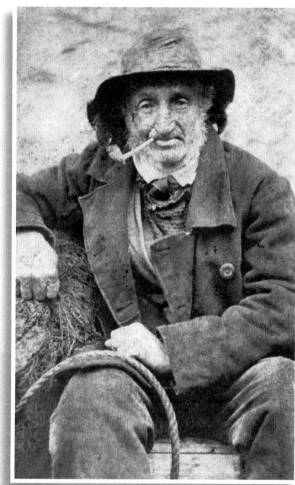

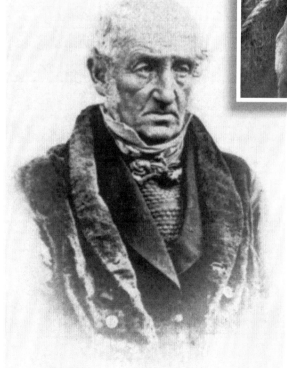

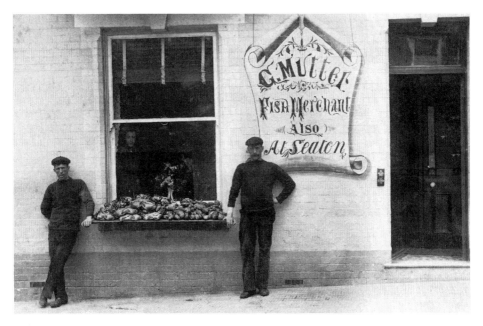

Mutter's fish shop in Fore Street, Beer, 1910. Here the crabs cost just 6*d* each – that's 2½p in today's money.

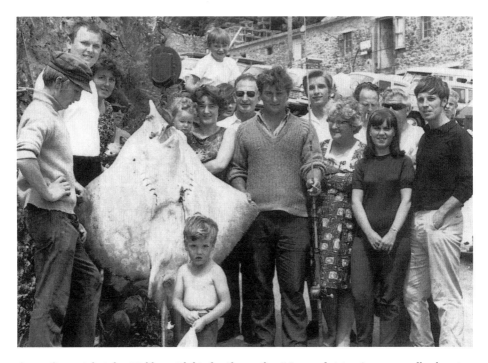

A very fine catch. John Wakley with his family, mother May, and sister Anne, proudly showing the massive skate which he caught in about 1960.

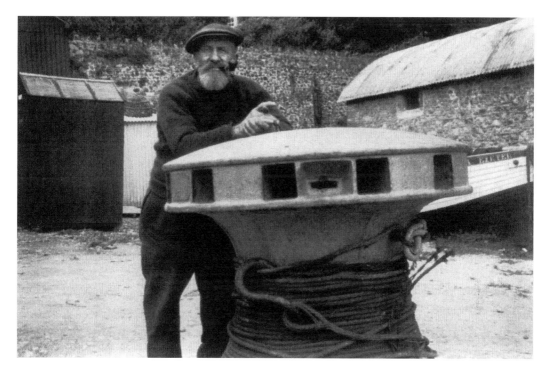

The big capstan and a Beer fisherman just after the First World War.

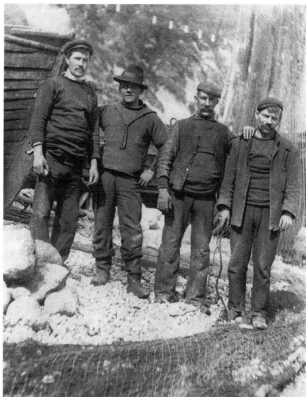

Some fishermen before the First World War. Norman Aplin (John Bull) is seen second from the left.

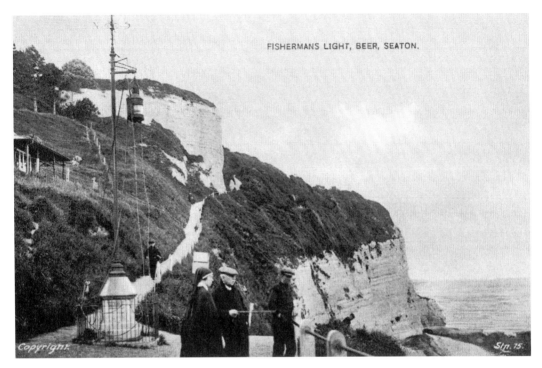

The Washbourne Memorial was presented to the village from the proceeds of a legacy from Mrs J.B. Washbourne (née Jane Bidney of lace-making fame) in 1895. She had left the sum of £100 with which the council decided to erect the Fisherman's Light. The position on the cliff top lines up with the church spire and was used as a navigational aid for the local fishermen when homeward bound. While the base and mast have been removed, the light remains in Beer church to this day. This picture is dated 1925.

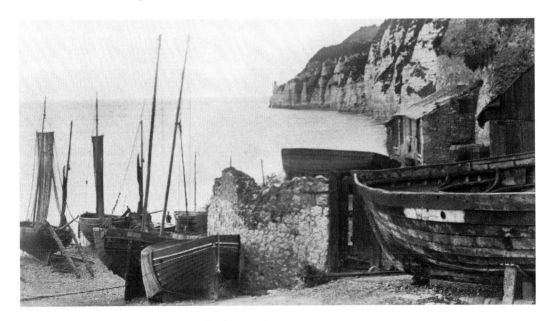

Boats pulled up beside and in Charlie's Yard in 1905.

Another large skate among the daily catch.
Les Boalch is the boy and 'Waddy' Woodgate
the fisherman in the boat, *c.* 1930.

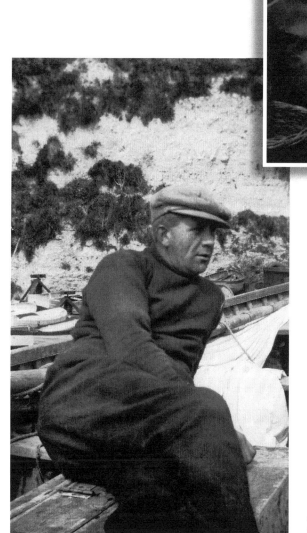

A Beer fisherman resting – note how clean
the sail is!

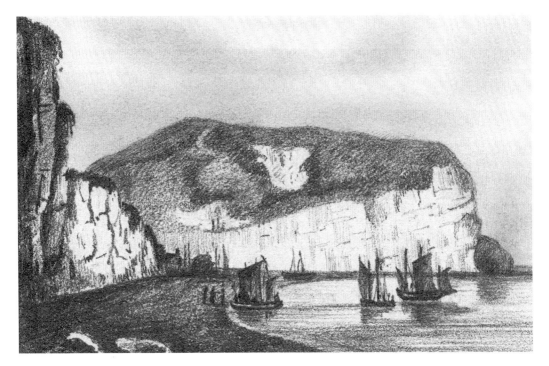

Beer harbour in 1829.

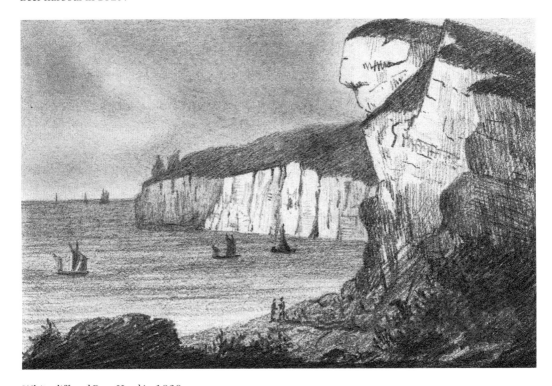

Whitecliff and Beer Head in 1829.

2

AROUND
THE VILLAGE

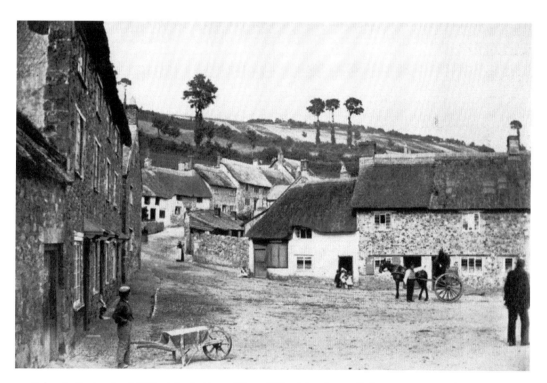

Taken in September 1875, at the bottom of Long Hill at The Cross, all the properties on the left of the picture still exist. Note the horse and trap and wheelbarrow in the foreground.

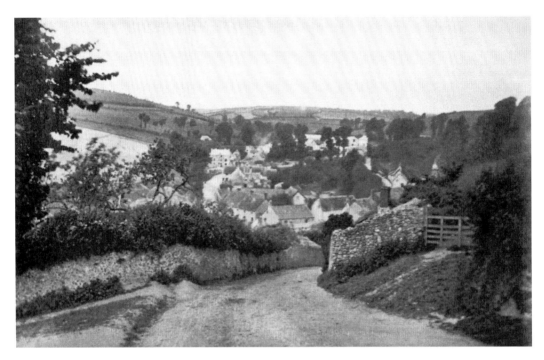

The entrance to Beer Village down Long Hill, September 1875.

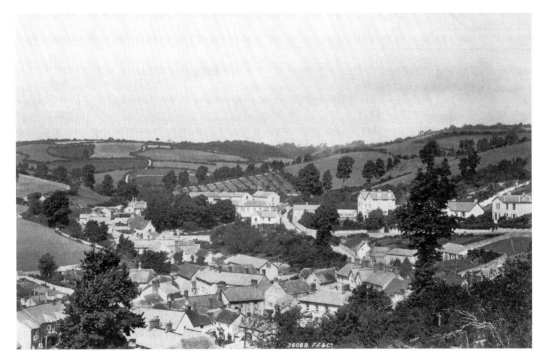

A general view of Beer in about 1910. The buildings in the centre at the top of the picture are Court Barton Farm with its fields behind. The narrow road on the left is winding its way to Branscombe.

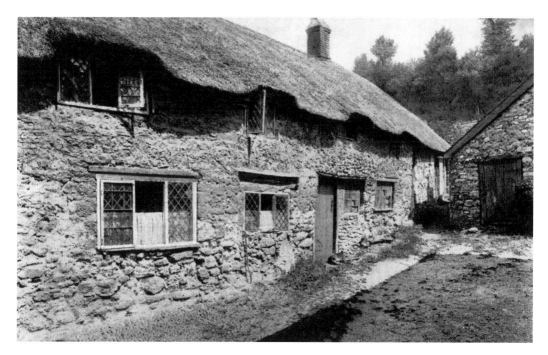

Jake Blackmore's Cottage, Steels Court, Beer, *c.* 1920. Jake Blackmore, a well-known Beer character, was a fisherman. Steels Court, which is now known as Otton's Court, was named after a shop owned by Dicky Steel which stood on the corner of Fore Street opposite The Dolphin Hotel.

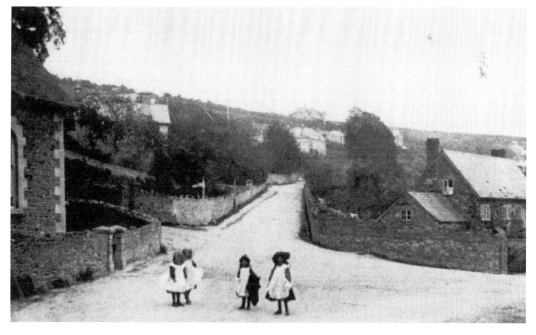

At the junction of New Road, Court Barton Hill and The Causeway with Spring Gardens Cottage and Beer Lower Infants School, *c.* 1900.

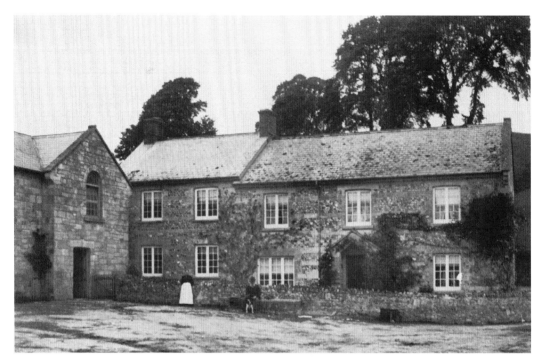

Court Barton Farm in 1900. Now the buildings have been converted into attractive properties, without destroying the exterior façades – all built of Beer stone.

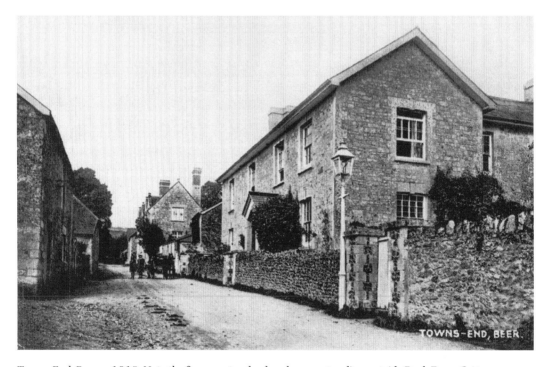

Towns-End, Beer, *c.* 1910. Note the fine gas standard and pump standing outside Rock Farm Cottage.

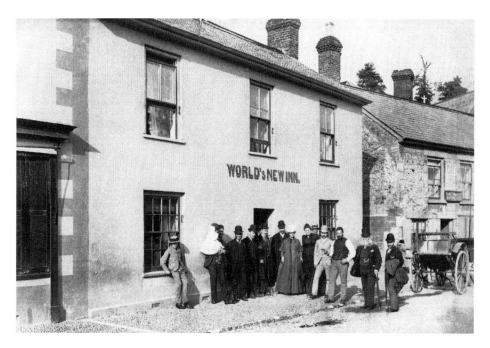

One of the earliest pictures of the village. The reason for the gathering of people is unknown, but dates from 1868. The pub (the New Inn) had been used by Jack Rattenbury. Miss Carrie World, who inherited the property from her father in early 1900, 'saw the light' and after a church service one Sunday went home and emptied all the cider, beer and spirits into the brook opposite and the inn was closed. It is now the Beer Newsagents.

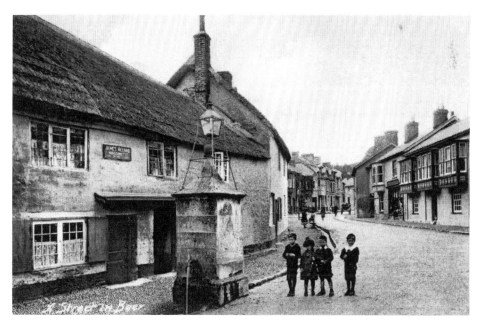

The water conduit with four small Edwardian children outside James Agland's property, now Sherbourne House. This picture dates from September 1911.

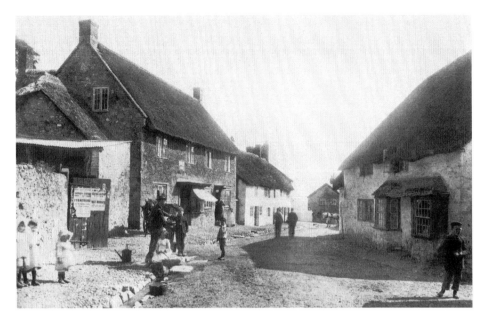

Looking down Fore Street, Beer, *c.* 1885. Photography was still sufficiently unusual to attract attention when this picture was taken over 135 years ago. The thatched cottages on the right were pulled down to make way for Beach House and the brook on the left supplied the village with a stream of pure water that flowed rapidly towards the beach.

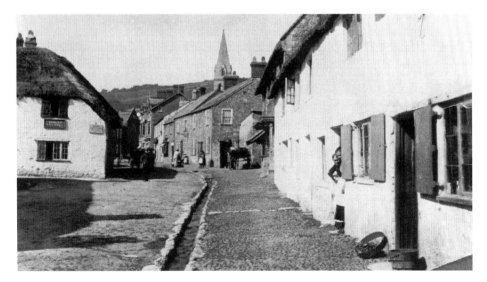

Another old picture of Fore Street towards the end of the nineteenth century (*c.* 1890). The village is an essential part of the English landscape, and the quaint, charming fishing village pictured here holds a special place in the heart of all Devonians. At the time of this photograph, Beer was mainly populated by fishermen, quarrymen and farm workers. Change came very slowly to them and the old village ways still remained. The folk of Beer then, as now, were warm-hearted people and strangers were always made welcome. Much has changed since the date of this picture. Newcomers now outnumber the true natives. Despite all, Beer people still remain the salt of the earth; their speech has not yet lost the rich Devon accent and they still retain the qualities of their forefathers.

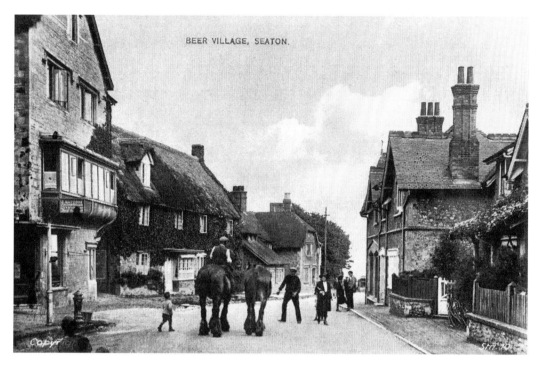

'I want a horse' could well be the caption of this photograph at the lower end of Fore Street in about 1920.

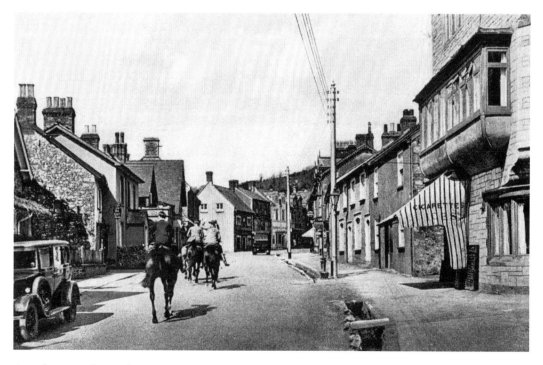

A car, horses and a coach in Fore Street, Beer, 1932.

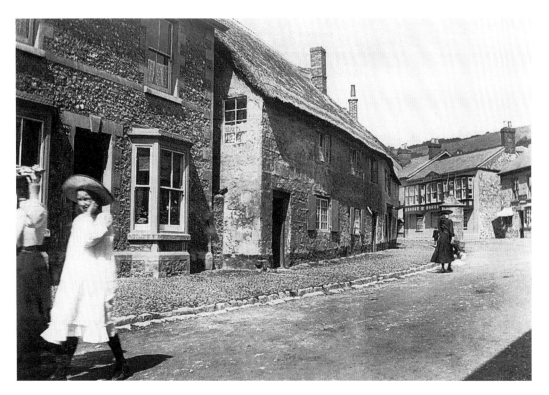

Fore Street, Beer, *c.* 1895. Photographs admirably convey scenes of long-past times and there is magic in this picture taken in Fore Street which brings a past landscape to life with its full range of evocations and associations.

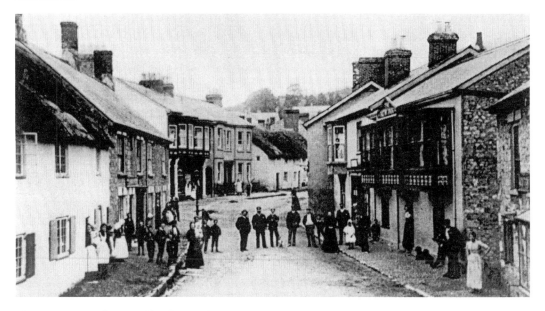

This unknown gathering of locals outside the New Inn in 1878 may have just celebrated the completion of the new St Michael's Church.

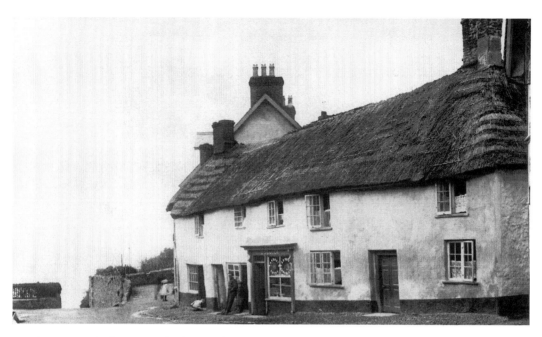

Fore Street, Beer, looking towards the sea. The thatched cottages were removed shortly after this picture was taken in 1902 to make way for what is now a car park.

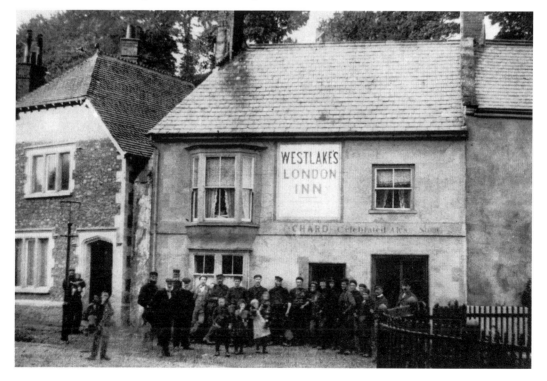

This picture depicts one of Beer's inns in 1897, the time of Queen Victoria's Diamond Jubilee, which the village celebrated in great style. Today the property forms part of Bay View Guest House.

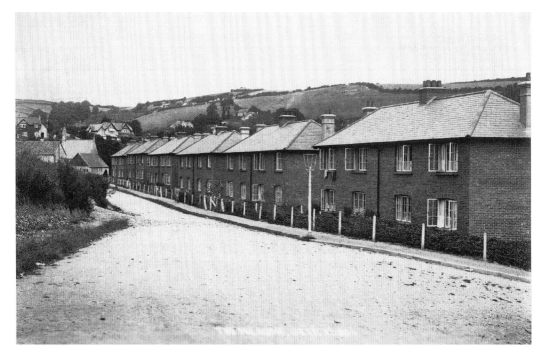

The newly-built Meadows in 1924.

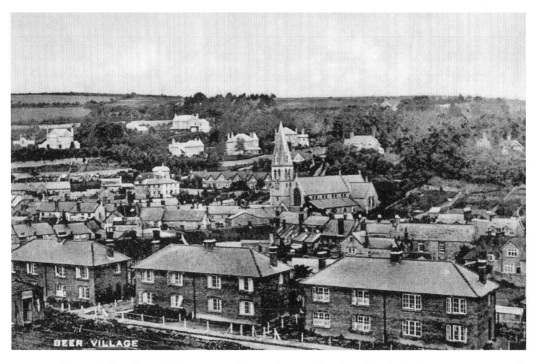

A pictorial view of the village looking across the Meadows to the church and fine houses on New Road, 1925.

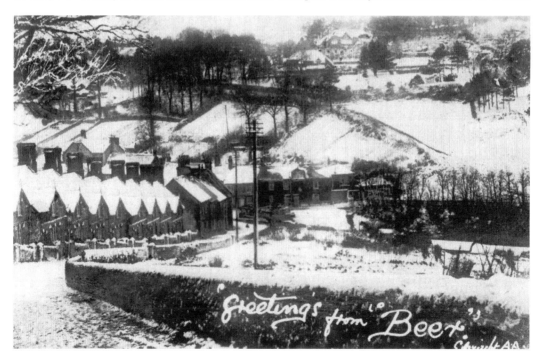

Fishermens Cottages, Beer.

An early view looking down the unsurfaced hill with the transport of the day, a horse and cart, across the road.

Greetings from "Beer"

How seasons change the appearance of a village. This shows snow in 1906 looking down Common Hill with the fishermen's cottages and allotments well covered.

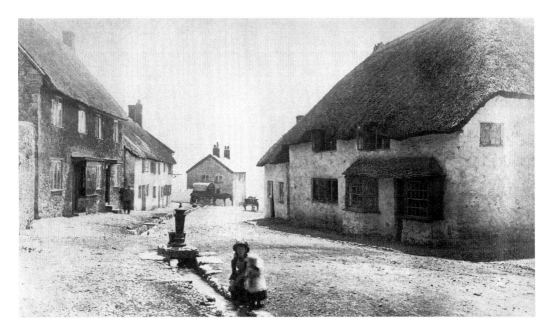

Beer Village, *c.* 1890. Views like this of people and houses that no longer exist seem to be inherently magical. In them the vanished past is made present again, yet the sense of the passage of time is overwhelming and we are reminded in pictures like this of how quickly things change.

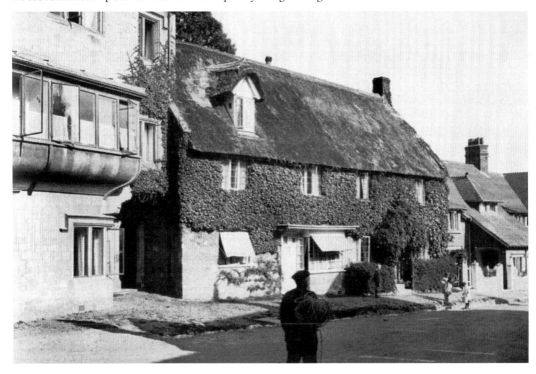

Beside the ever-flowing brook is Marine Cottage at the lower end of Fore Street. This photograph is dated 5 July 1921. How its appearance has changed over the past ninety years.

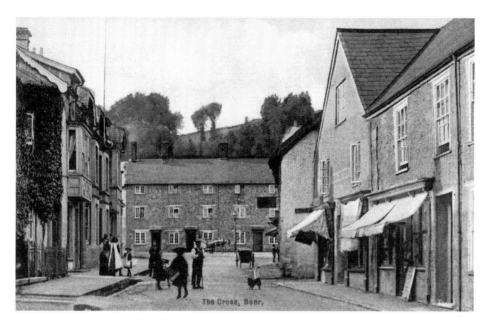

The Cross in 1910. The three-storey houses were built in 1664 of flint stone from Beer Common. Although Beer is famous for its lace and fishermen, another industry once flourishing but now obsolete was the making of gun flints. Before the invention of the percussion cap, many thousands of gun flints were made every year out of flints embedded in the chalk cliffs and local manufacturers had large government contracts for the Army and Navy.

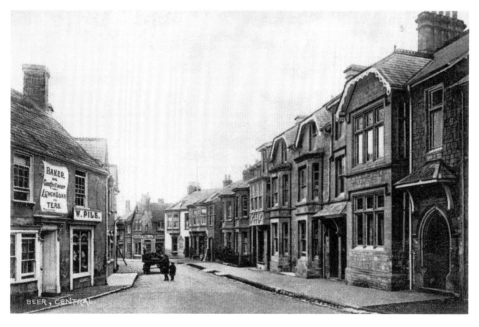

Fore Street looking down from The Cross with W. Pile the baker's shop in a prominent position. The village was very self-sufficient for just about everything up to 1950.

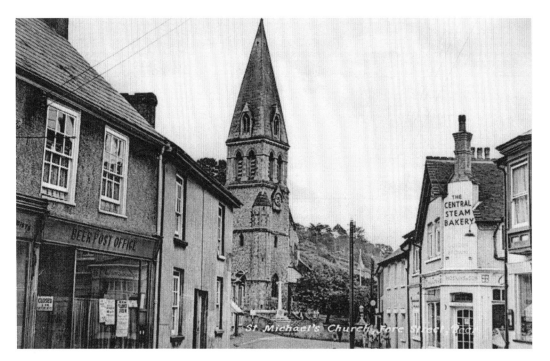

This picture was available as a postcard in 1948 and illustrates the village street with two essential shops and its fine church.

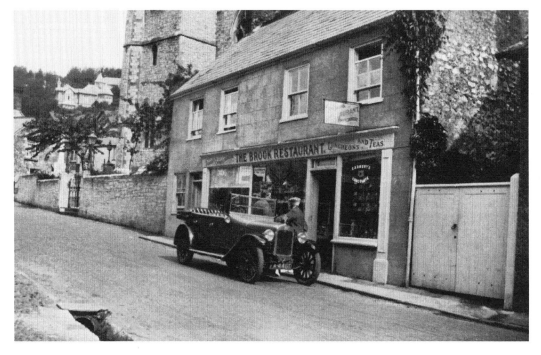

This fine motorcar parked outside the Brook Restaurant, owned by Mr Stapleton, visited in 1929. There were no yellow lines or traffic wardens for motorists to worry about in those early days!

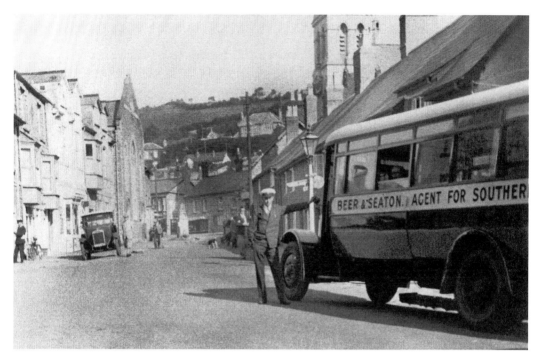

The local Beer/Seaton bus – the driver standing by the vehicle is Jack Grater.

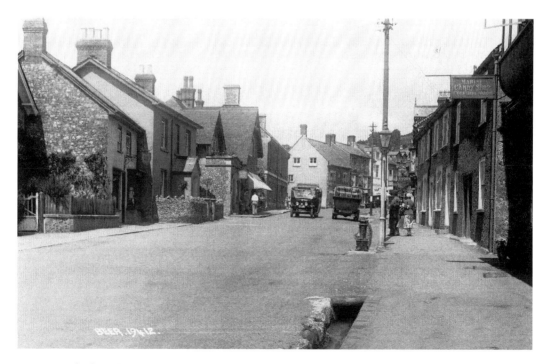

Marine candy shop, the Lace Shop and two fine examples of charabancs in Fore Street in the late 1920s.

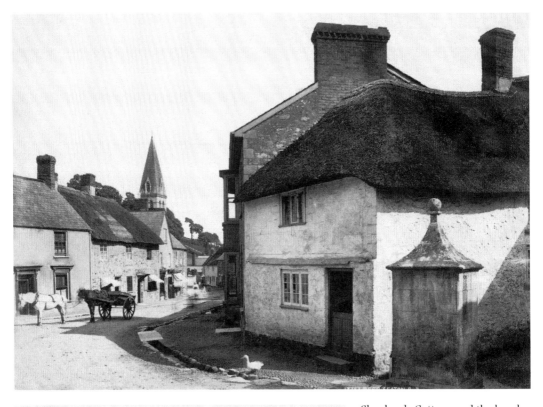

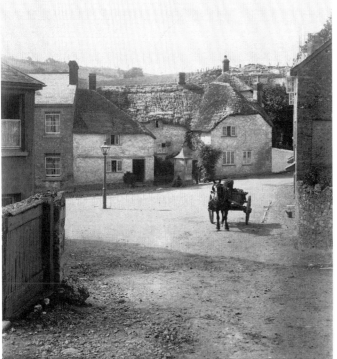

Shepherds Cottage and the brook, *c.* 1900. The open stream flowing down one side of the main street is known as Beer Brook. This brook, supplied with water from a spring near Bovey House, has never been known to run dry, and no locally born boy worth his salt can be called a 'Beer Boy' until he has fallen into it. One of the conduits made from Beer stone is pictured here and these were supplied for the villagers to draw water. They were built in 1832 as a gift from the Lord of the Manor's wife – Lady Rolle.

The Cross with the village pump in the background and Shepherds Cottages, *c.* 1890.

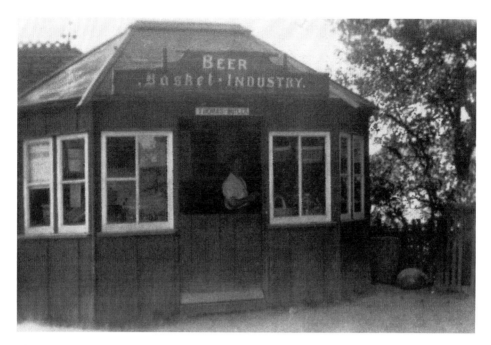

This picture is the only known illustration of Thomas Butler's basket shop. It was taken in 1928 by Mr Arthur Morton. This site is now the shop of the RNLI.

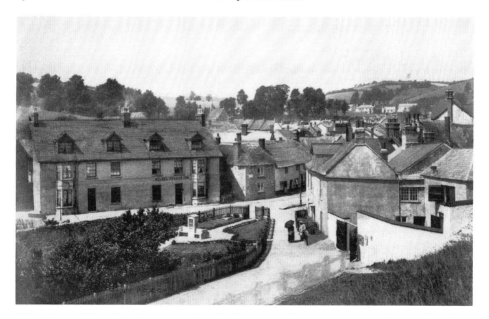

This picture of Beer dates from over a hundred yeas ago. The monument standing on the plot in front of the Anchor Hotel commemorates the artist Hamilton Macallum, who for many years made Beer his home. When he died in 1896 at the age of fifty-five, this memorial and stone seat was erected by his friends. The thatched cottages to the right of the Anchor were knocked down at a later date and the site is now a car park. Much has changed in Beer since that day long ago, but the village still remains one of the best-loved in Devon.

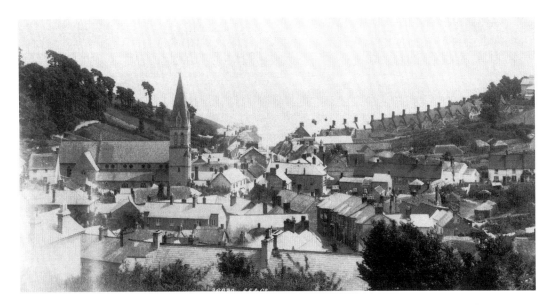

A general view of Beer, *c.* 1890. Beautifully situated in a deep, narrow glen, Beer was a fishing village formerly in the tithing of the Civil Parish of Seaton. In November 1894 it was formed into a separate parish under the Local Government Act of the same year. At that time Lord Rolle was Lord of the Manor and the main landowner.

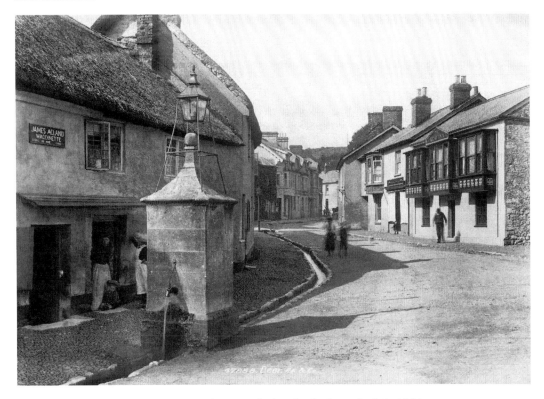

Fore Street, *c.* 1900. Note the water conduit over the brook which was built in 1838.

Looking down Church Hill in 1899 towards
St Michael's Parish Church.

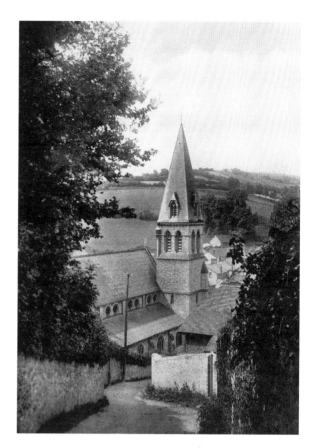

Fore Street showing the New Inn in 1895
with its window boxes which still remain
some 120 years since they were installed.

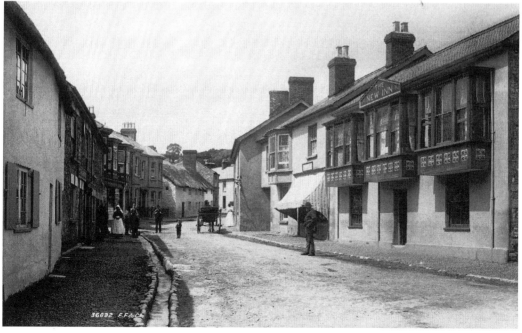

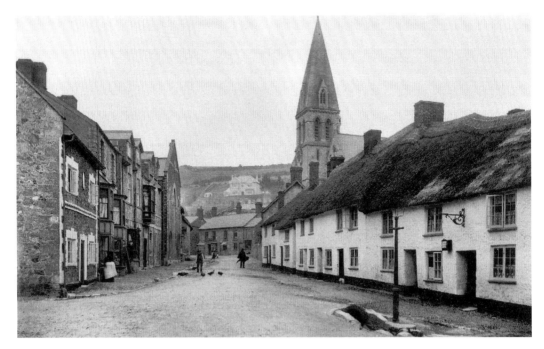

Fore Street looking towards the church. The road was not surfaced, but the street was kept in good order as can be seen from the cottages which exist today some 110 years on from when the picture was taken.

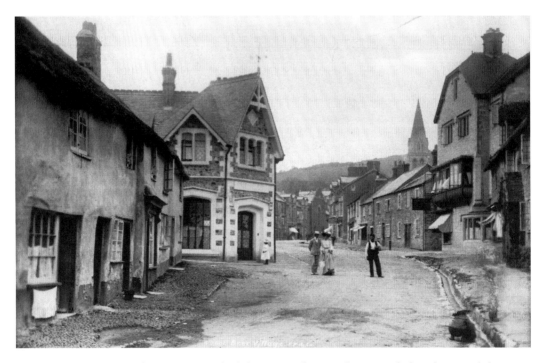

Fore Street, Beer, 1904. The cottages on the left are now the site of a car park, but the rest of the street remains the same. The church spire was removed in the 1960s.

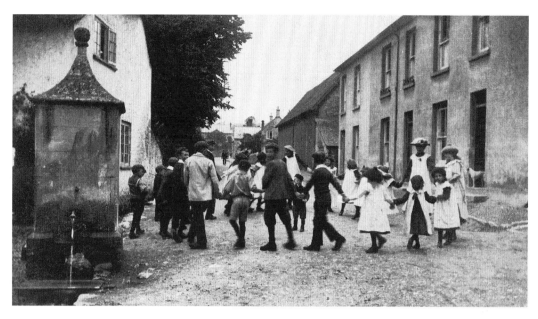

Here on a sunny morning a century ago the children of Beer can be seen in this delightful picture playing 'Ring-a-Roses' in the main street opposite Shepherds Cottage. It was still a time when children could play in safety, but obviously this would not be possible these days.

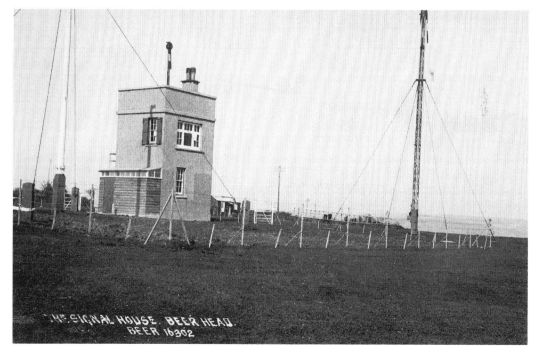

The Signal House or Coastguard lookout station on Beer Head, 1910. A twenty-four-hour watch took place here from the time of smuggling until the mid-1930s, when a smaller building nearer the highest point was erected and used until the late 1980s.

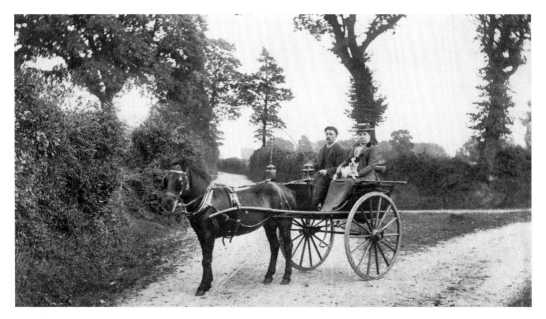

Mr and Mrs Westlake at Bovey Cross out for an afternoon drive in 1890.

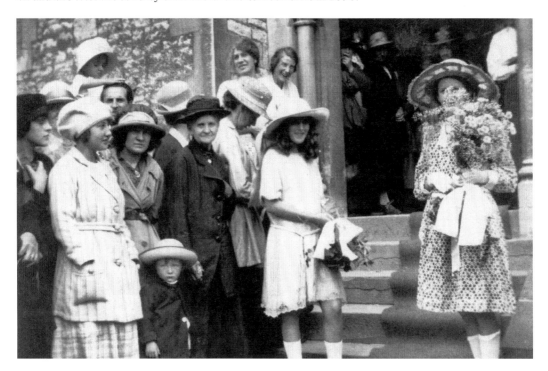

A wedding in Beer, *c.* 1929. An unknown photographer has successfully captured the feeling of excitement on the faces of the ladies, young and old, who were waiting for the bride to arrive at the parish church. The two girls standing on the steps were obviously bridesmaids and look slightly self-conscious. The expression on the face of the little boy standing in the front wearing the large hat seems to suggest he would like to be anywhere but there. The bride is unknown but she might have been a member of Dr Tonge's family.

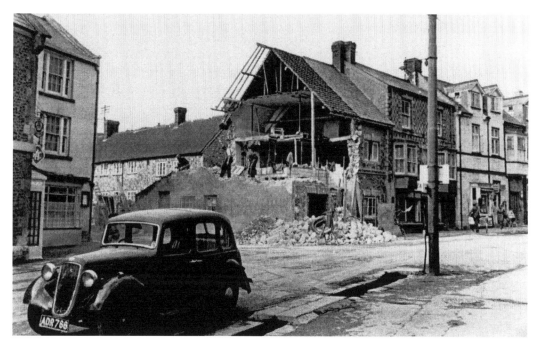

The demolition of what was affectionately known as Gills Corner. Note that there are no health and safety regulations in place for either the workmen or the approaching pedestrians. The replacement building is Pegasus Cottage.

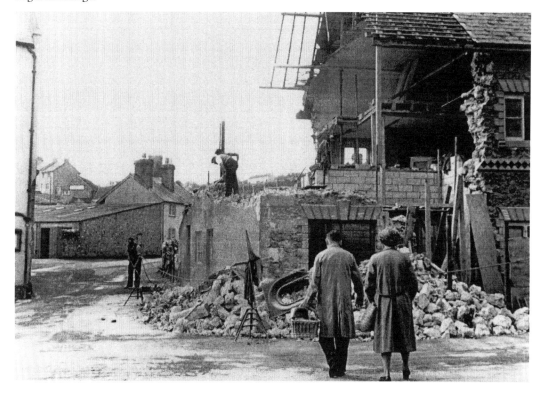

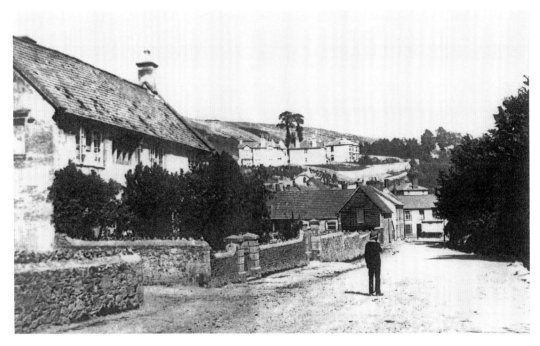

The Causeway and entrance to Beer's main street in 1900. The property on the left of the picture is Starre House, which dates back to the mid-seventeenth century.

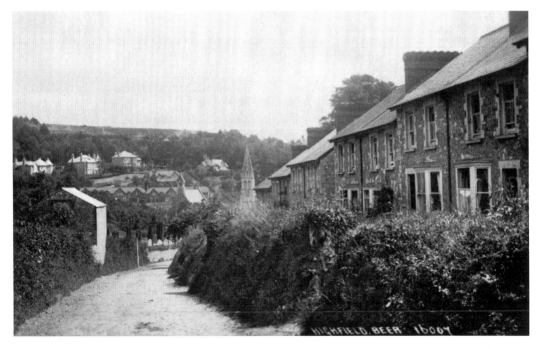

The development of Clapps Lane took place in the late 1920s and early 1930s. The photograph shows Highfield Terrace on the right of the picture. The church spire and the cemetery are in the lower centre with the fine buildings on New Road – quite a contrast all in the one picture.

3

SCHOOL & CHURCH

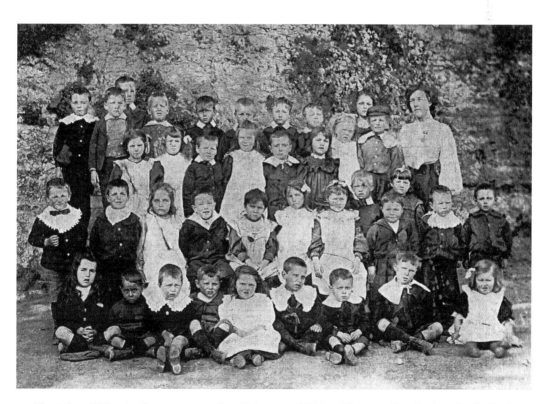

The Infants' School at Beer was opened on 19 January 1874 and, being a Church of England school, was visited by the vicar, the Revd Mr H. Vyvyan three days later. This picture was taken in about 1874/5 with the mistress being Susan Hawkins. In 1883 Miss Elizabeth Pike, aged twenty-four, took charge of the school; a position she held for the next thirty-nine years until 12 April 1922. The infants' school amalgamated with the higher school (or upper school as it was sometimes referred to) in 1931 when both moved into a new school building.

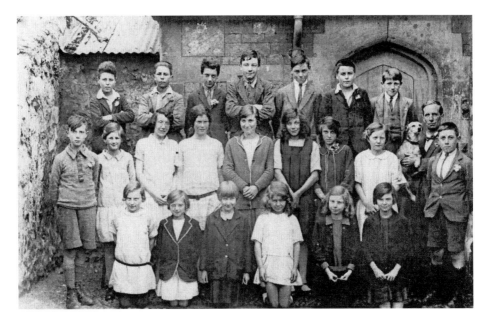

Mr W. R. David took charge of Beer C of E School on 1 October 1918 and had 89 children on the school roll initially. He remained headmaster for thirty years and made a huge contribution to the village in many other organisations in which he was involved. He commanded great respect throughout the village. This picture was taken in the early 1920s.

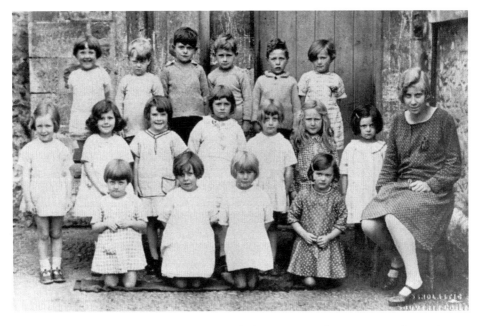

Miss Beryl Ham, the teacher in this photograph, became a supplementary teacher at the age of eighteen in 1927 at the infants' school. For the next forty-nine years she continued as the infants' teacher, having had hundreds of pupils (including the author) pass through her class. This photograph dates from 1930.

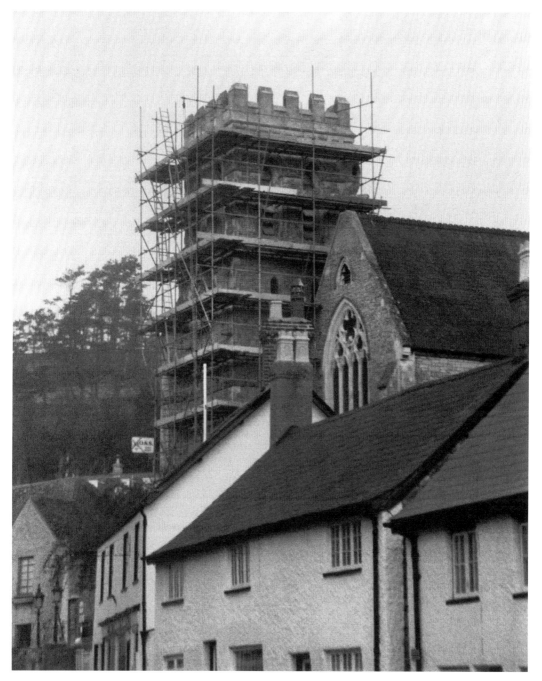

The Parish Church of St Michael at Beer was a gift from Lord Rolle. It was built between 1876 and 1878 and was consecrated by the Bishop of Exeter. Until December 1905 it was a chapel-of-ease to Seaton, and became independent ecclesiastically when the then Curate in Charge, of eighteen months, the Revd Mr Andrew Hollis, became Vicar of the Parish of Beer until January 1939. During these thirty-five years served by Revd Mr Hollis there were five Kings of England and a world war. This photograph shows the spire having been removed in 1963 prior to the scaffolding being dismantled.

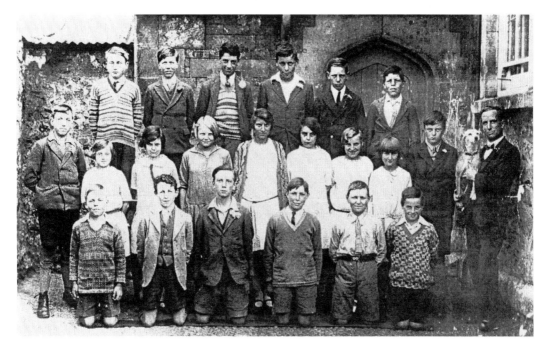

Do you recognise any of the pupils? It seems unfair to pick out the odd one for fear of upsetting so many who are now senior citizens. These photographs were taken in 1931/2.

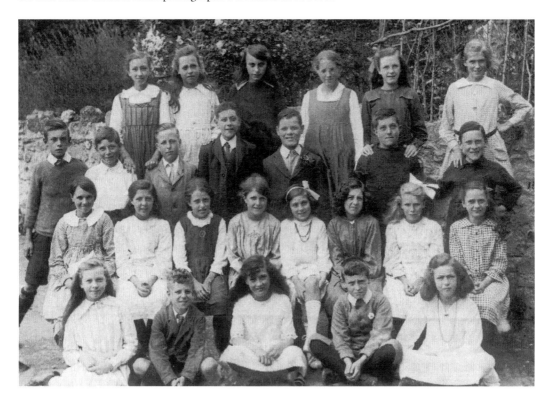

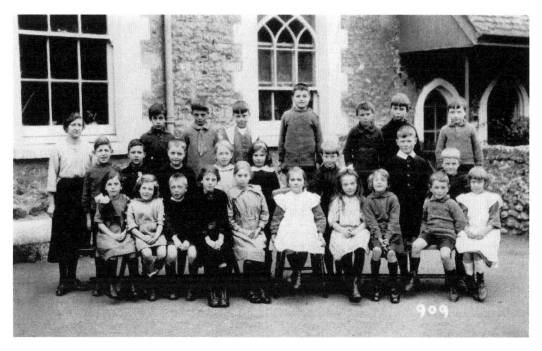

Another picture of Beer School in the early 1930s at the newly built combined infant and junior premises.

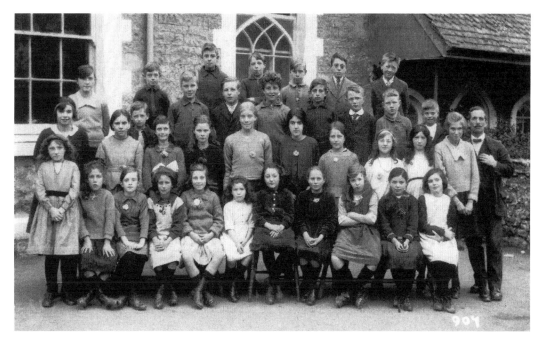

Beer schoolchildren in the mid-1930s.

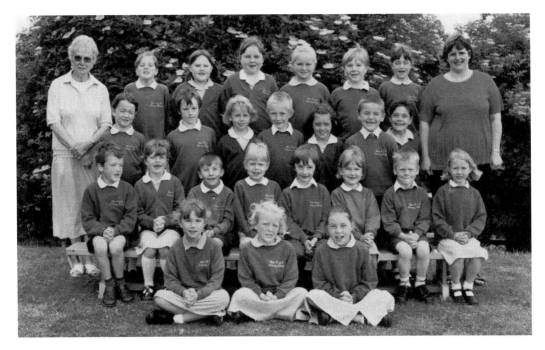

Beer School class 4 in 2001.

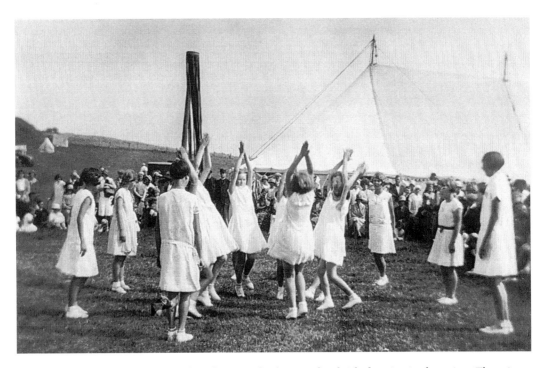

Beer Flower Show, August 1931. This photograph of Beer schoolgirls dancing is charming. There is no feeling at all that this picture was pre-arranged because it has life. It is a snatch of social history that gives the viewer a strong feeling of being there.

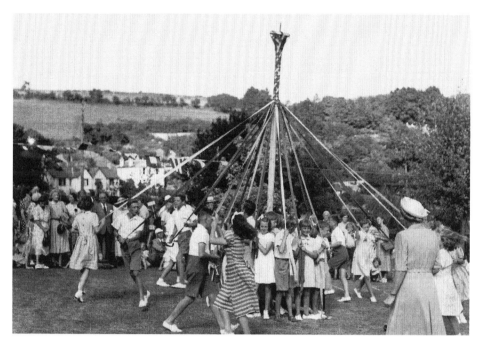

Maypole dancing at Glenmure, Barline, Beer. Ted Gosling took this picture for the local press in 1957. The maypole was a feature of many village activities and Miss Beryl Ham, the Beer Primary School mistress who taught generations of Beer children the dance, is standing on the right with her back to the camera.

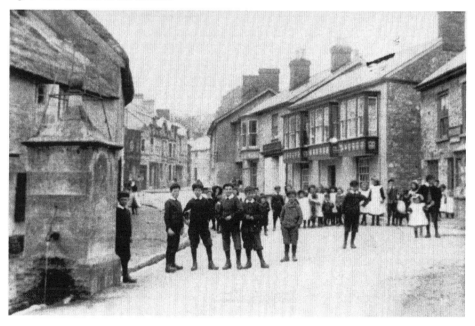

Fore Street, 1904. This photograph of typical Edwardian children posing for the camera in a Beer street is so rich in information and so attractive in its mix of facets and atmosphere that it compels attention.

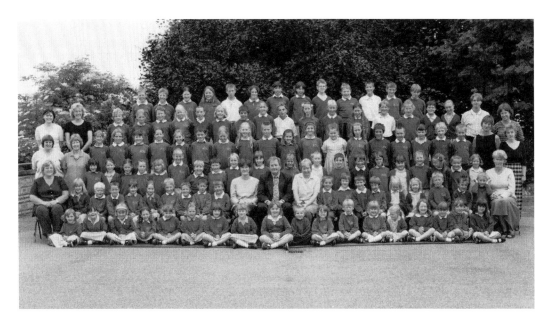

Beer School millennium photograph, 2000.

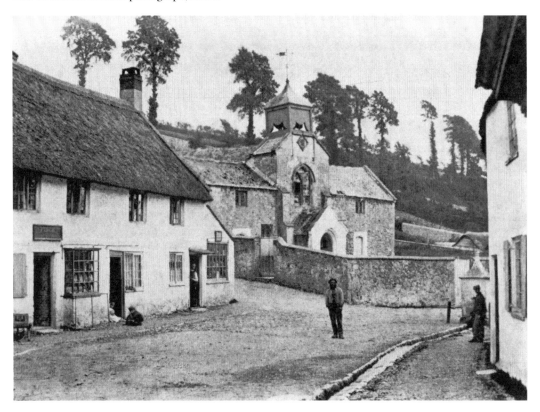

This picture is the old Beer church, or chapel-of-ease. It was demolished in 1876 to make way for what is now St Michael's Parish Church, which was consecrated in 1878.

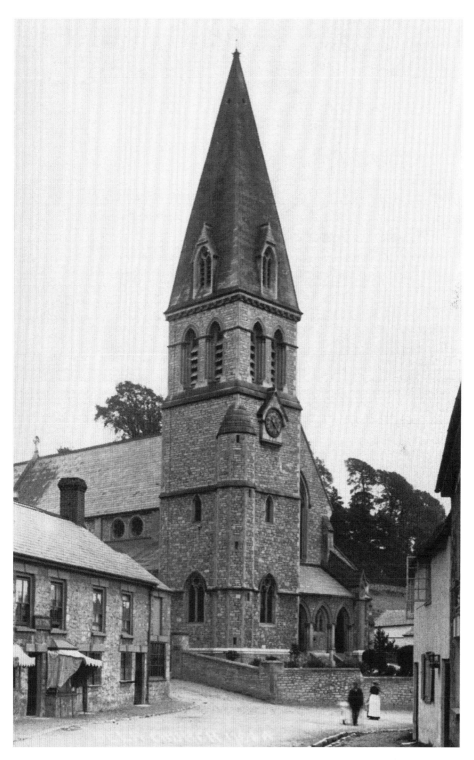

Beer Parish Church, *c.* 1912.

These two photographs are of the Beer war memorial in commemoration of the men of the village who gave their lives in the First World War. The unveiling service was held on Sunday 13 July 1919. A particularly black day for the village was on 31 May 1916 when five young men lost their lives at the Battle of Jutland.

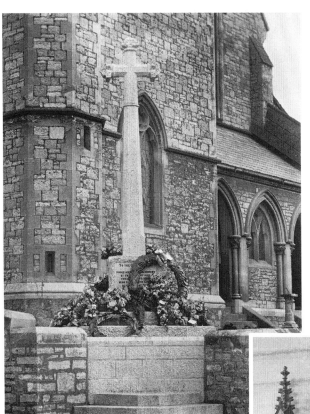

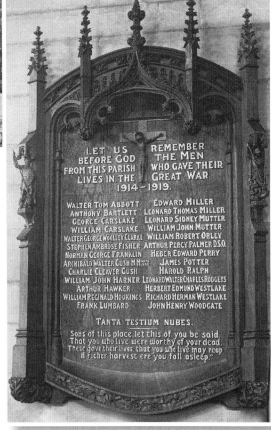

LET US REMEMBER
BEFORE GOD THE MEN
FROM THIS PARISH WHO GAVE THEIR
LIVES IN THE GREAT WAR
1914–1919.

WALTER TOM ABBOTT	EDWARD MILLER
ANTHONY BARTLETT	LEONARD THOMAS MILLER
GEORGE CARSLAKE	LEONARD SIDNEY MUTTER
WILLIAM CARSLAKE	WILLIAM JOHN MUTTER
WALTER GEORGE WOOLLEY CLARKE	WILLIAM ROBERT ORLEY
STEPHEN AMBROSE FISHER	ARTHUR PERCY PALMER D.S.O.
NORMAN GEORGE FRANKLIN	HEBER EDWARD PERRY
ARCHIBALD WALTER GUSH M.M.	JAMES POTTER
CHARLIE CLEAVER GUSH	HAROLD RALPH
WILLIAM JOHN HARNER	LEONARD WALTER CHARLES RODGERS
ARTHUR HAWKER	HERBERT EDMUND WESTLAKE
WILLIAM REGINALD HOOKINGS	RICHARD HERMAN WESTLAKE
FRANK LUMBARD	JOHN HENRY WOODGATE

TANTA TESTIUM NUBES.

Sons of this place, let this of you be said
That you who live were worthy of your dead:
These gave their lives, that you who live may reap
A richer harvest ere you fall asleep."

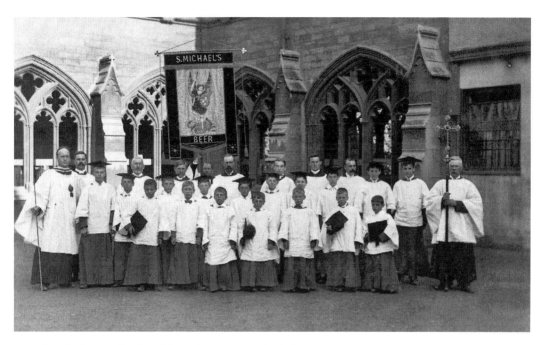

Beer church choir at the choral festival at Exeter Cathedral in June 1906.

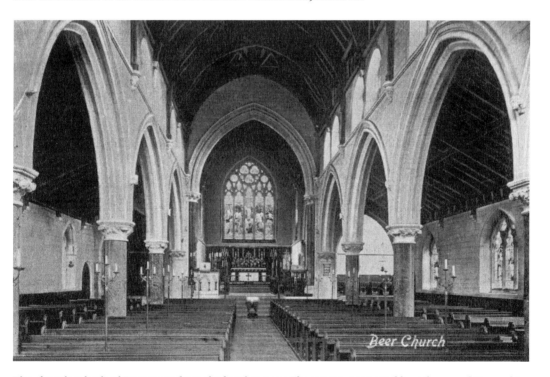

The church is built of Beer stone from the local quarry. The nave is supported by columns of Devonshire marble and there is a fine stained-glass east window, which was also a gift from the Hon. Mark Rolle at Ascensiontide in 1889.

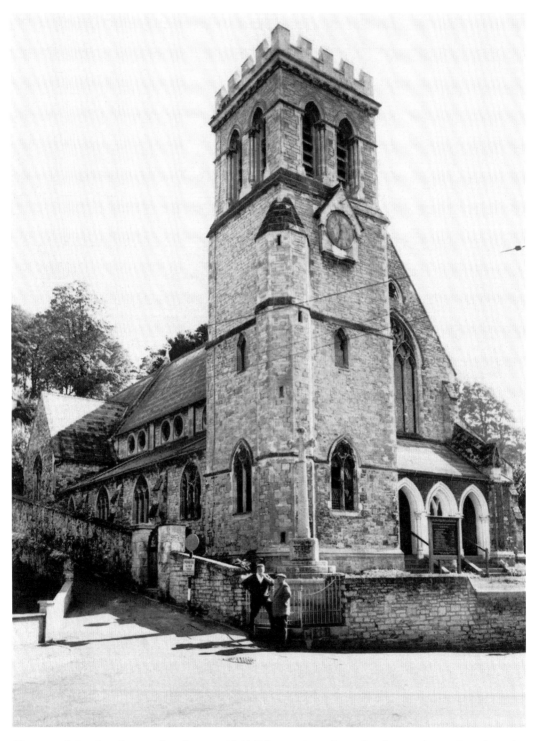

The spire of the church was taken down in 1962/3 having been deemed to be unsafe, resulting from the explosion of a land mine during the Second World War.

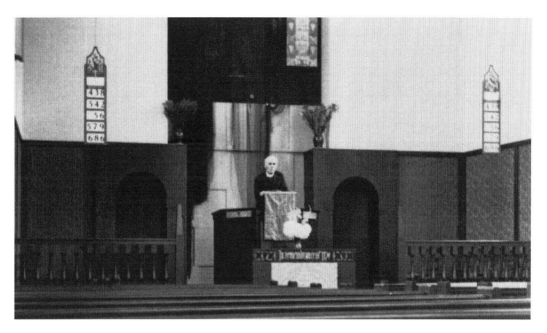

An unusual photograph of the Congregational Church in 1933 where the Revd Mr Tucker was the minister at the time.

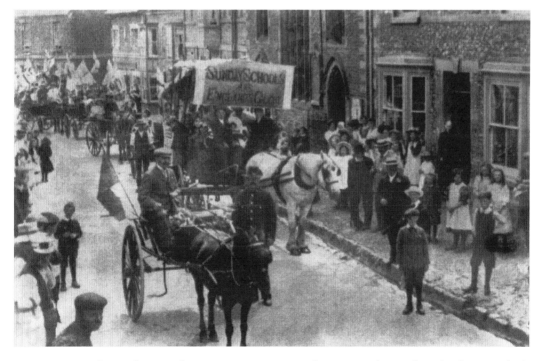

Fore Street turned out to be a very busy street in June 1902 as here we see the Sunday School outing which left the village for Bovey House. Note the children in their Sunday best in anticipation of an exciting day's tea party.

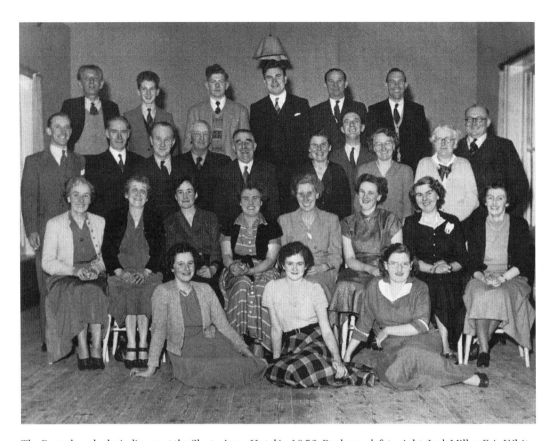

The Beer church choir dinner at the Shute Arms Hotel in 1952. Back row, left to right: Jack Miller, Eric White, Norman Lambert, Eric Westlake, Colin Jones, Bob Jones. Middle row: Francis Eyles, Roly Burningham, Mr Tartlin (organist), Bill Blackmore, Bill Collier, Monica Dormer, Lionel Bastone, Irene Bastone, Mrs Blackmore, the Revd Mr W.H. Dormer. Third row: Mrs Tartlin, Mrs Burningham, Molly Payne, Mary Eyles, Beryl Ham, Doreen Bastone, Sheila Jones, Avril Butchers. Seated on floor: Mary Butchers, Vera Collier, Joy Bartlett.

4

BEER LACE

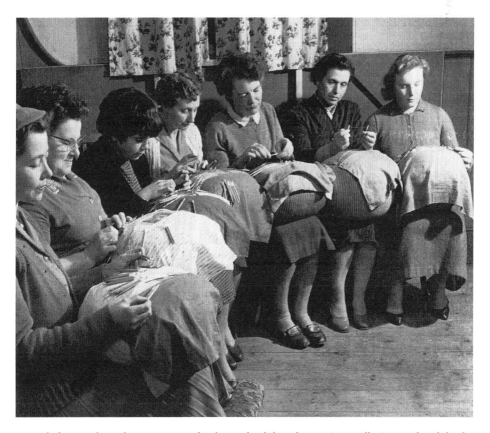

Beer ladies at a lace class. Note Maud Orley and Sybil Anderson (née Miller) second and third left, and Mrs Sergeant third from the right, *c.* 1956.

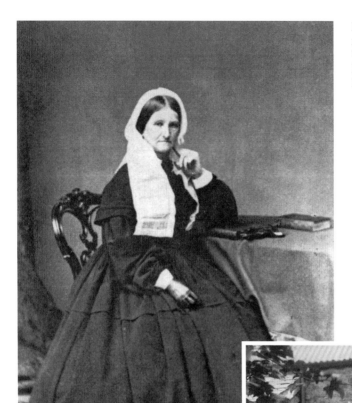

Miss Jane Bidney of Beer, who received the order to decorate Queen Victoria's wedding dress with Beer lace. She was later invited to the Royal Wedding.

Mrs Woodgate at the age of eighty-six. She helped make Queen Victoria's wedding flounce in 1839. She was probably the most famous of Beer's lace makers.

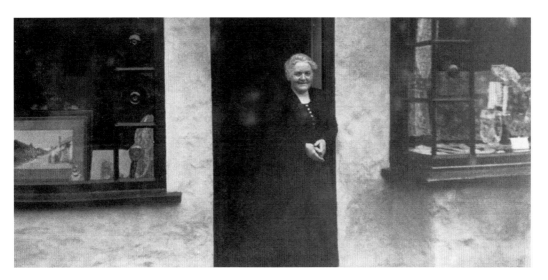

Mrs Ida Allen was the lady at the Lace Shop in Fore Street, Beer, for some fifty years from 1906. During that period she had many famous people visit the shop including the Duke of Connaught (Queen Victoria's youngest son), Sir Winston Churchill, Dwight D. Eisenhower (later President of the USA), Jack Hobbs (the cricketer – on his honeymoon), and Freddie Mills (at the time of his visit the World Middleweight boxing champion). Mrs Allen's son recorded his wish that his mother had kept a visitors book of the people who had visited her shop over the years.

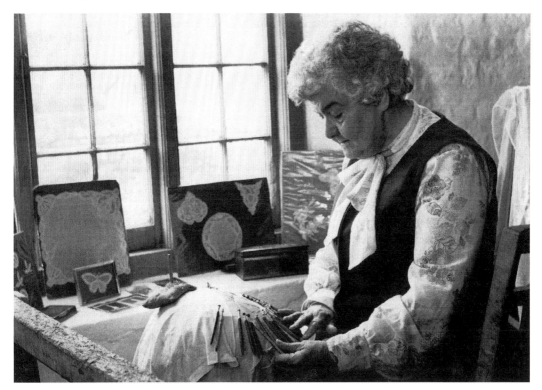

Mrs Allen's daughter Biddy at work.

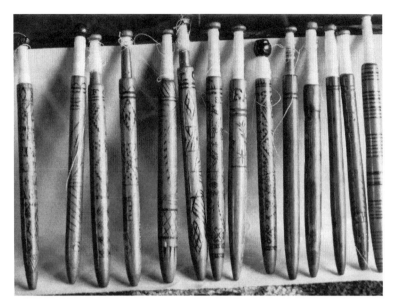

A close-up of some of the bobbins used by the lace makers in Beer. These bobbins are hand-made, very old and covered with patterns and inscriptions to their loved ones.

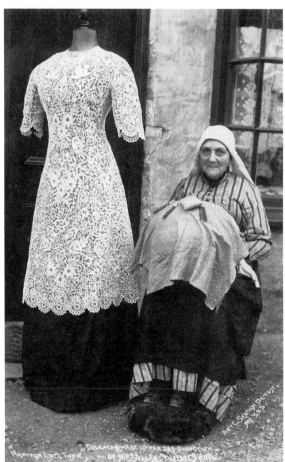

This magnificent lace dress, dated 1914, took hundreds of hours to make under the direction of Mrs Allen.

This photograph, taken outside the Lace Shop at Beer, is of Mrs Winifred Lambert and a friend visiting from Cape Town in 1954. The little boy is David Boalch.

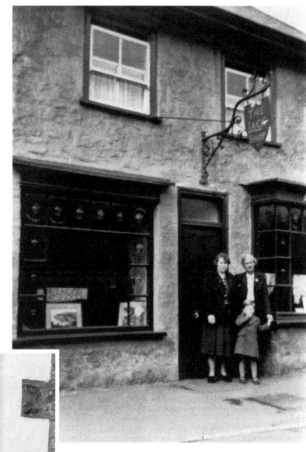

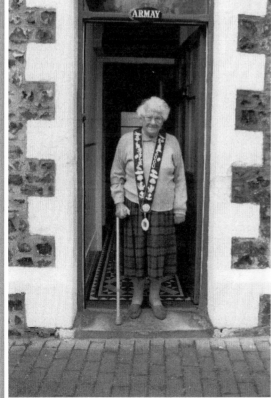

Mrs May Wakley on her ninetieth birthday. This lady is wearing the Chairman of Beer Parish Council's ceremonial collar, which is made up of lace pieces made at May's weekly lace class for the Millennium celebrations.

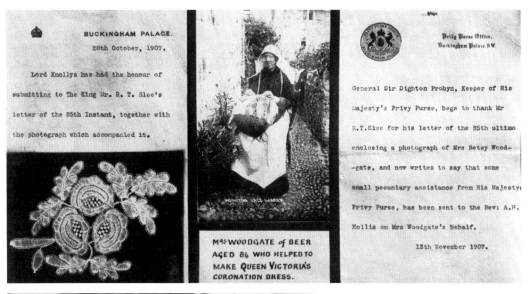

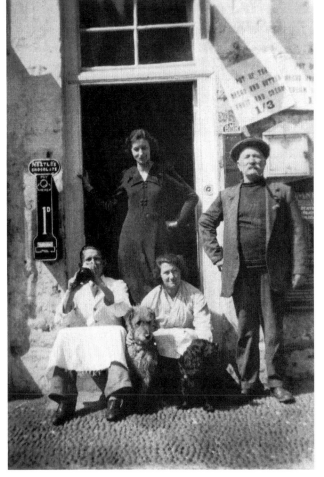

Interesting correspondence on Mrs
Woodgate's behalf with Buckingham
Palace in 1907.

Outside the Anchor Hotel in 1939
are Margaret White and Baker Beale
standing with an unknown chef
and May Wakley. Note the chocolate
machine on the wall where its contents
could be purchased for one old penny
and, as the sign states, a cream tea for
1s 3d – 6p in today's money.

5

VILLAGE PEOPLE & SPORTING EVENTS

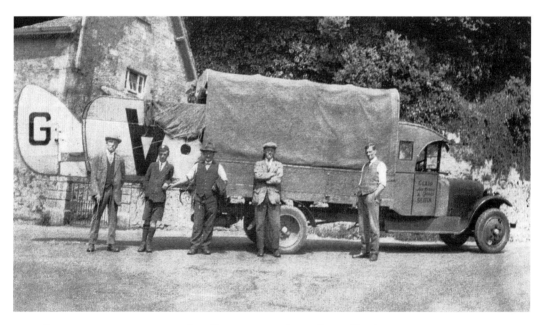

There was great excitement in the village in 1926 when a de Havilland aeroplane crash landed on Beer Common. Clapps Transport were given the contract to return the plane to the de Havilland works and in the picture you can see the wings with a part of the tailplane sticking out of the rear of the lorry. The people in the picture are from left to right: Mr Tidcombe, Stanley Oborn, local garage owner Mr W.L. Oborn, Bill Keate who drove the lorry and Harry Clapp who was the owner of Clapps Transport.

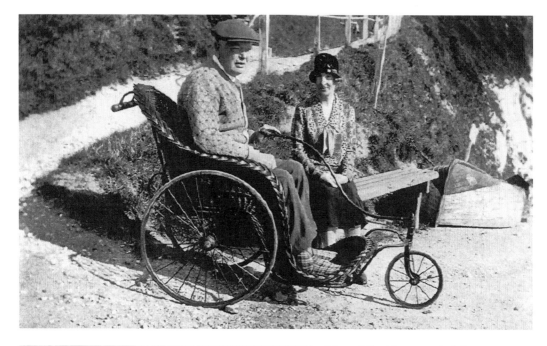

Mr and Mrs Morton on holiday at Beer in 1928. Note the excellent wheelchair. This photograph was used as the couple's Christmas card for that year.

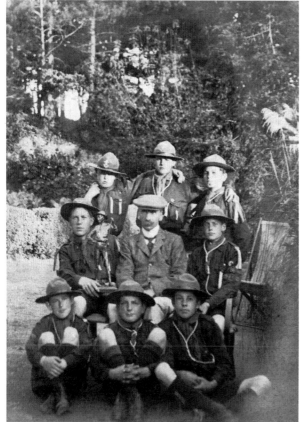

Dr Tonge, the Beer doctor, is pictured here with some of the Beer Scouts in 1914. The boy to Dr Tonge's right is holding a small statue so this could have been an award presentation ceremony.

John Thomas Hamilton Macallum, artist, born 22 March 1841, died 23 June 1896. The monument erected in his memory portrays the love, affection and admiration in which this fine artist was held.

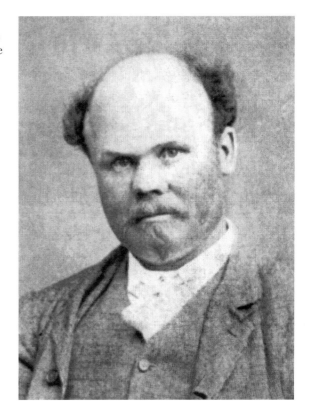

Two generations of Macallums beside the monument which was unveiled in 1897.

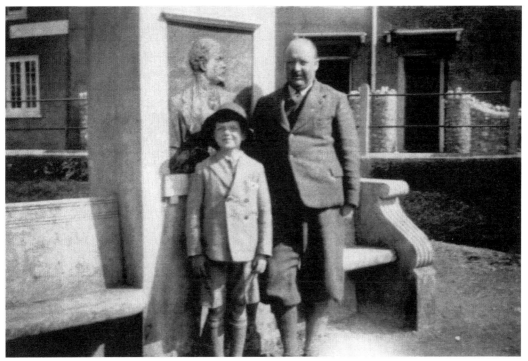

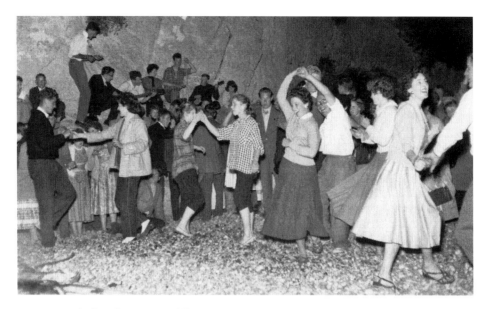

Dancing on the beach in 'Tom Tiddlers Hole' (now completely filled to the roof with pebbles) in 1956. Among the gathering are Monty and Penny Laptin, 'Wookie' Michael and Ruby Collier, and Wendy and John Underwood. Peter Northcott is in the centre.

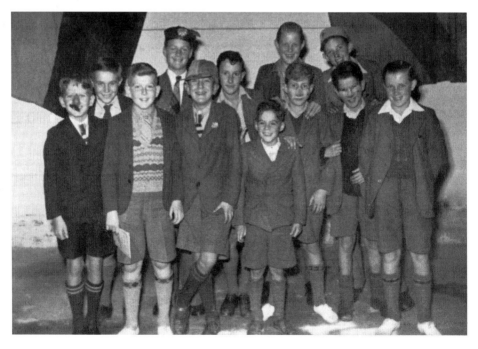

There are still a number of people living both in the village and neighbourhood from the days this picture was taken in 1949 at Pioneer Garage in the New Cut, Beer. Front row, left to right: Eric White, Alan Rooke, Norman Lambert, Ian White, John Miller, Norman Rooke, Elwyn Collier, Stuart Barrett, Mick Barrett. At the back: Barry Merrett, Bob Aplin, Bernard Bond.

Tom Barrett with his prize pumpkin preparing for the annual pumpkin fair, which is held in September each year. This photograph is from about 1960.

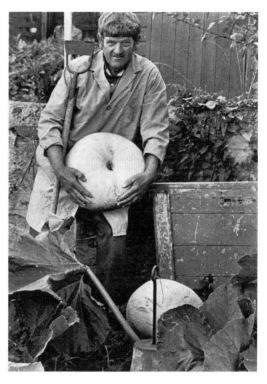

After the Second World War and before the general advent of television, most families gathered in the evening around a wireless set. The new Light Programme attracted a huge audience and programmes such as *Down Your Way* and *Twenty Questions* and entertainers such as Wilfred Pickles had over fifteen million listeners a week for his programme *Have a Go*. The people of Beer are seen here gathered in the school to enjoy the excitement when Wilfred Pickles broadcast his programme live from the village in about 1950. There are many well-known faces in the picture, including Percy Westlake, Rupert Aplin, Peter Bartlett, Beryl Ham, Gwen Westlake, June Laptin, Anne Collier and Wendy Orley.

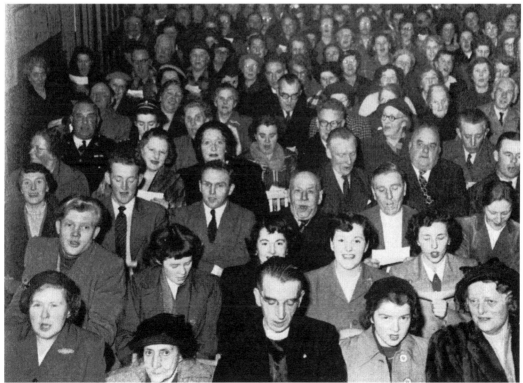

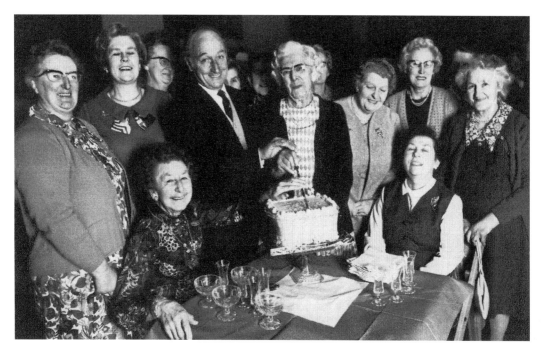

The Beer branch of the British Legion was very active after the Second World War. This picture depicts a birthday celebration of the branch in 1967. Pictured are Jean Blackmore, Mary Chapple, George Bastone, Mrs Perkins, Winifred Lambert, Winnie Stokes, Mary Harvey. Seated are Mrs White and Mrs Longhurst.

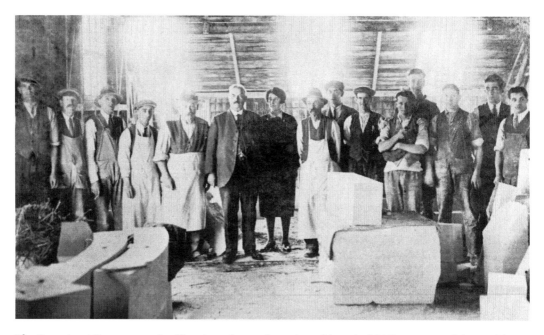

The Quarries at Beer were a significant employer of people and here in 1925 are some of the workforce, including Eddie Rodgers and Elija Tyrell, the manager, and his wife. Note the size of the blocks of stone which had been cut for the workshop.

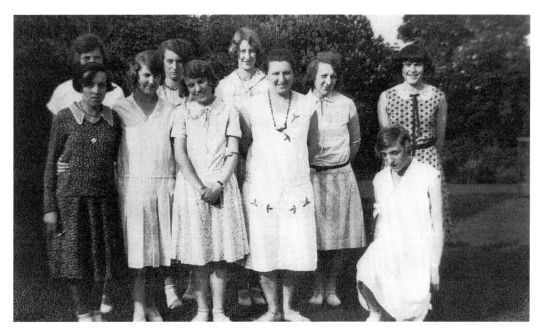

This expressive photograph charged with life and atmosphere shows the Beer W.I. folk dancing team who posed for this picture on 4 June 1930.

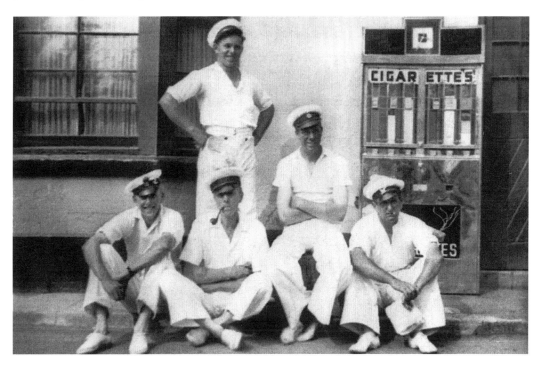

This picture was taken in happier times before the Second World War outside the Anchor Hotel. Standing is David Chapple (who was sadly killed in the war) and seated are, left to right, Tony Driver (also killed in the war), Dougie Orley, Fred Newton and Jack Westlake.

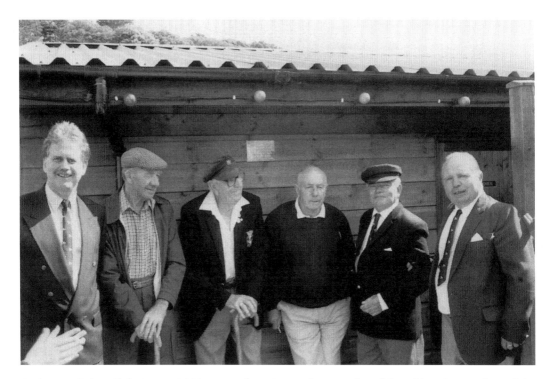

At the Beer Sailing Club, August 1992. Pictured are Commodore David Boalch and founder members of the club in the 1930s, Fred Newton, Dougie Orley, Raymond Driver, along with President Archie Lockyer and Hon Secretary Robbie Driver.

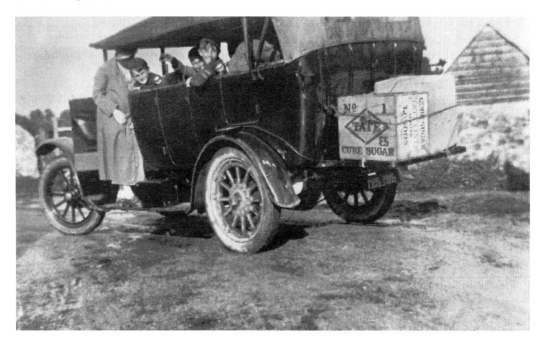

Beer Cubs setting off to camp in about 1929. The camp was held at Weston Gap.

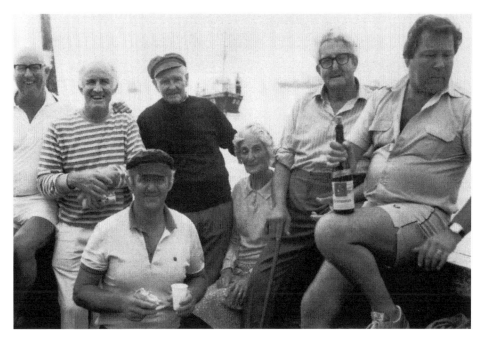

The Beer pumpkin show, 29 September 1993. Ken Westlake was the auctioneer for the produce that was gathered for the show apart from the main exhibits. Great rivalry and secrecy is practised in case of sabotage. Ken, on the left, is seen with John Ward and Steve Ward at the Beer Social Club.

A happy gathering on Beer beach. Left to right are Michael Collier, Elwyn Collier, Cecil Gush, Mrs Gush, Ern Westlake, Brian Northcott, Peter Bartlett.

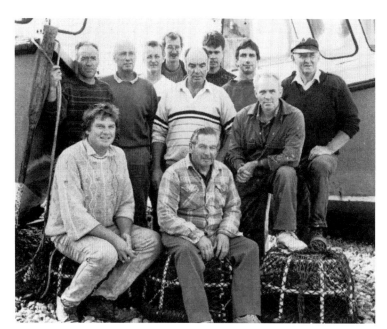

Seen here are David Newton, Jim Chapple, Jim Newton, Gary Aplin, Ali Green, Peter Bartlett, Roy Newton, Cyril Newton, Kim Aplin, Alan Westlake.

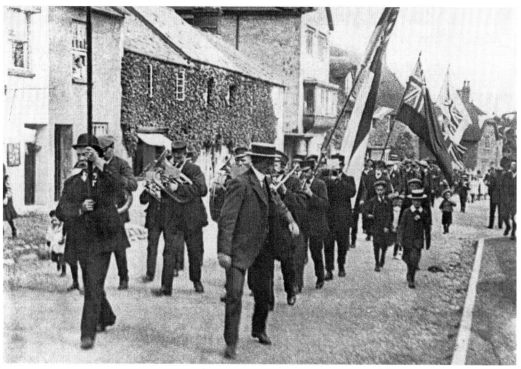

Beer Club Walk, 1908. About this time nearly all the men who lived in the village belonged to a Friendly Society which had the admirable objective of assisting its members in time of sickness and providing a sum of money at death. The annual club day was an event much anticipated by the villagers. It commenced with the club walk, led by a band which members followed carrying banners and poles festooned with bunches of flowers which they waved about with much merriment.

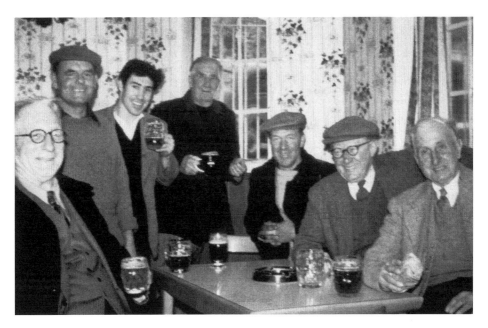

In the Anchor Inn enjoying a jar and no doubt a good tale or two in about 1950 are Tom Boalch, Rupert Aplin, -?-, Herman Bartlett, Fred Newton, Walter Hanker and Gerald Restorick.

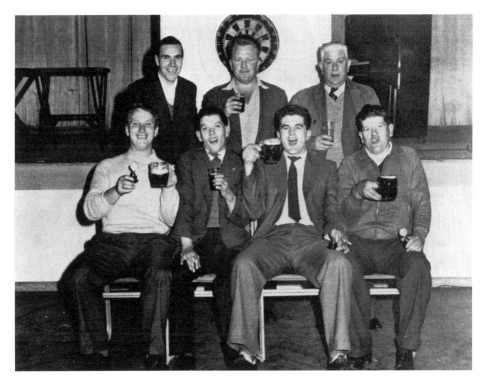

A winning darts team in 1956. Back row, left to right: John Purse, Ken Westlake, Les Mutter. Front row: Jim Chapple, Stuart Barrett, Monty Laptin, Tom Barrett.

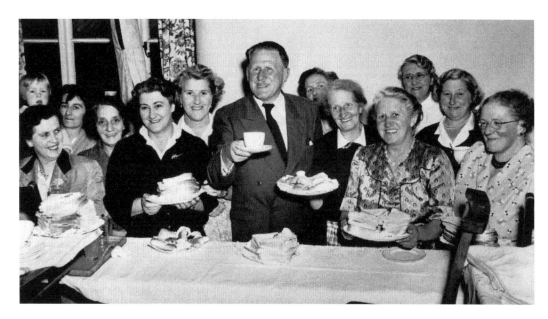

The BBC wireless broadcaster Stuart Hibberd is seen here in 1951 with the ladies of the Beer Women's Institute, including Eileen Critchard, Joan Frankland, -?-, Mary Wakley, Mrs Mutter, ? Longhurst, Mary Harvey, Gladys White, Alice Frankland, Elsie Miller and Gwen Westlake.

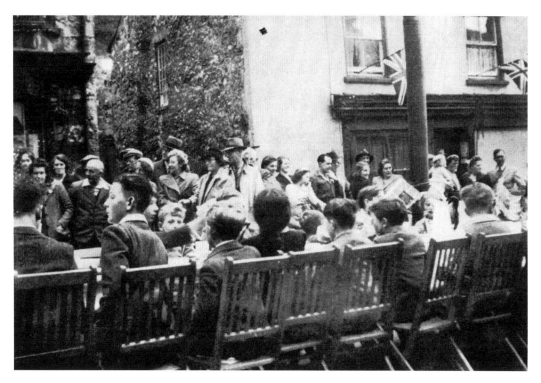

The June 1946 Peace Victory tea party in Fore Street outside the Lace Shop. The little boy facing the camera is Norman Lambert and the bigger boy second from the left is Peter Bartlett.

Mrs Florence David, the headmaster's wife, on her 100th birthday. She lived to be 104 and had lived at Marine House in Fore Street for forty or so of those years.

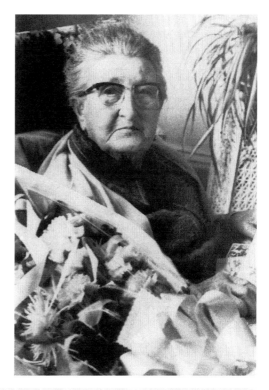

Beer, 1926. Fisherman William Rowe demonstrates the use of the cork life-jacket at a life-saving apparatus drill in the presence of the local inspector of coastguards.

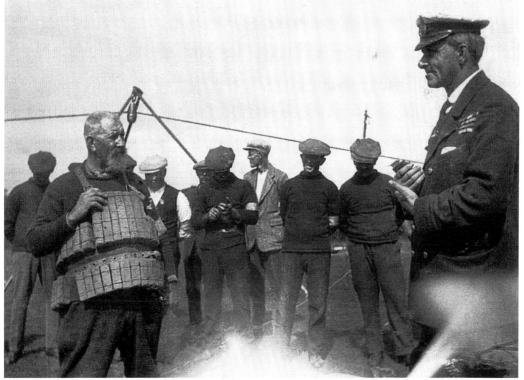

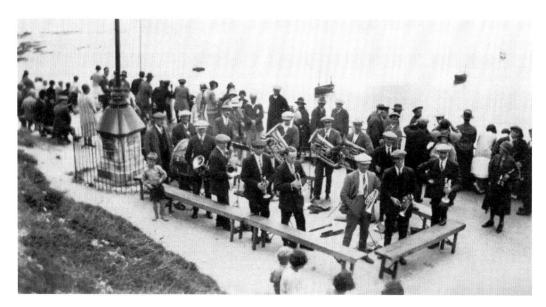

The Beer Band was disbanded in 1936, but hitherto had played at most of the village functions on high days and holidays including Beer Regatta. This photograph shows the band assembled on the clifftop in 1924.

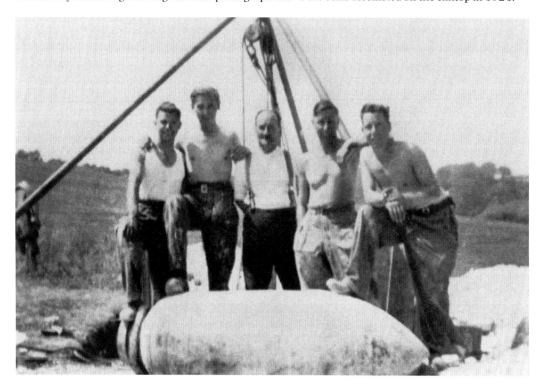

The bomb disposal units of the Royal Engineers had the thankless task of digging out and making safe the many unexploded bombs that fell on England during the Second World War. Pictured here during May 1944, the men of one such unit are working on the unexploded bomb in Paizen Lane, Beer. Local garage owner Mr W.L. Oborn can be seen standing in the centre of the team.

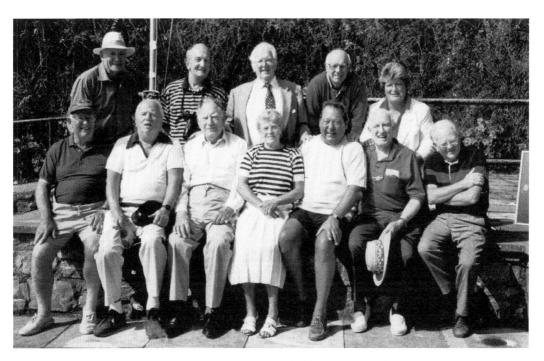

Beer Regatta has always attracted great interest and is held on the second Thursday following the first Monday in August each year. It is a great honour to be invited by the committee to open the event, there having been some interesting people in the past, including the round-the-world yachtsman Sir Alec Rose in 1969 and Alan Minter the World Boxing Champion in 1982. This picture was taken on Regatta Day, 12 August 1999, when the author officially opened the proceedings, and the photograph features predominately 'Beer Boys' with the Regatta President and Chairman. Back row, left to right: Eddie Bond, Ian White, Norman Lambert, David Burridge, Gayle Chapple (chairman). Front row: Michael Collier, Alan Bricknell, Alf Boalch, Mary Davy, Brian Northcott, Elwyn Collier, George Hookings.

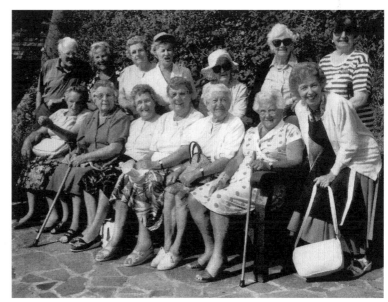

A fine array of Beer ladies at the 1998 Regatta, accompanied by George Hookings. Seen here are: -?- , Barbara Rogers, Mary Byrne-Jones, Eileen Critchard, Dorothy Burridge, Mary Good, Betty Dare, Mrs Diamond, Irene Bastone, -?-, Myrtle Mutter, May Wakley and Rita West.

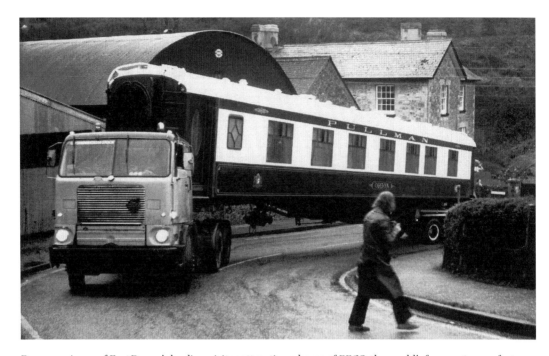

Pecorama is one of East Devon's leading visitor attractions, home of PECO, the world's foremost manufacturer of model railway track, and the location of the award-winning Beer Heights Light Railway. Superbly crafted layouts in many gauges of track greet visitors to the PECO railway exhibition, while outdoors the 7¼-inch gauge miniature railway carries passengers on a mile-long ride through flower-filled gardens, steep-sided cuttings and a long, dark tunnel. On site the 'Orion' Pullman car gives you a glimpse into the past to the days of luxury travel. The 'Orion', which now serves coffee, tea, cream teas and cakes, caused a stir in the village of Beer when it arrived after its long journey from Wolverton. The 'Orion' in all its glory is seen here entering Mare Lane from The Causeway, a gradient of 1 in 5, on 8 February 1978.

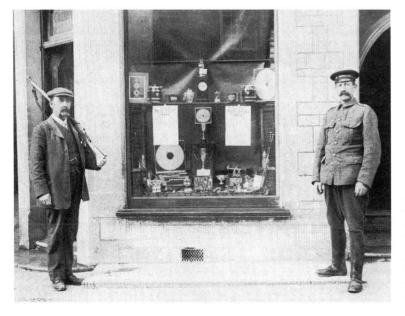

Beer Miniature Rifle Club was formed in 1908 and this photograph was taken outside Colebrook House in 1909 with James Perkins and his shop, illustrating the prizes for that year's club competition.

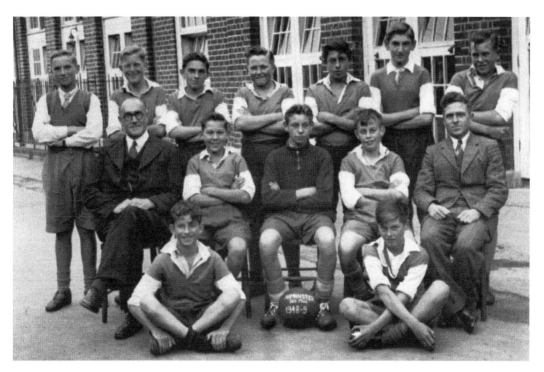

This is the Axminster Secondary School football team of 1948/9 with no less than six Beer Boys. Among the back row are Jim Chapple, Bob Aplin, Ken Westlake, Tim Bartlett. Beside Mr H.B.Tolchard, the headmaster, is Brian Northcott, Billy Head and Master Ted Denham.

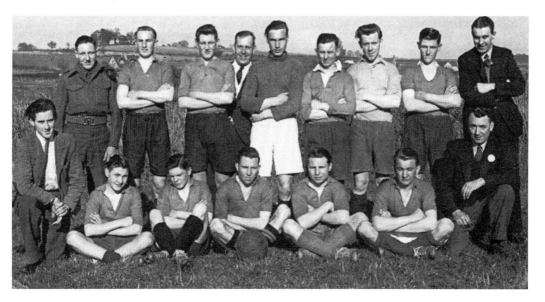

Season 1947/8 at Ilminster where Beer lost 6–4 in the Perry Street Charity Cup. Back row, left to right: Tom Abbott, John Newton, Sid Carter, 'Coco' Hawker, John Graham, Norman Westlake, Ted Newberry, Ted Barrett, 'Doc' Clarke. Front row: John Underwood, Tony White, Basil Agland, Ted Perry, Robbie Driver, John White and the coach driver.

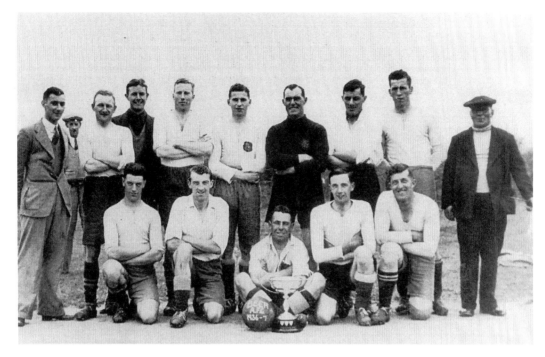

Beer Albion first team in 1937 having won the Axminster Hospital Cup which they are proudly displaying. The team at that time played in the Perry Street League.

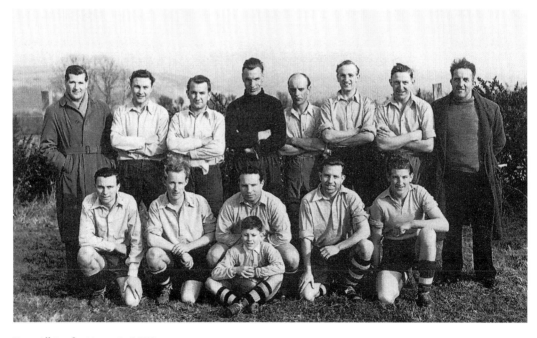

Beer Albion first team in 1950.

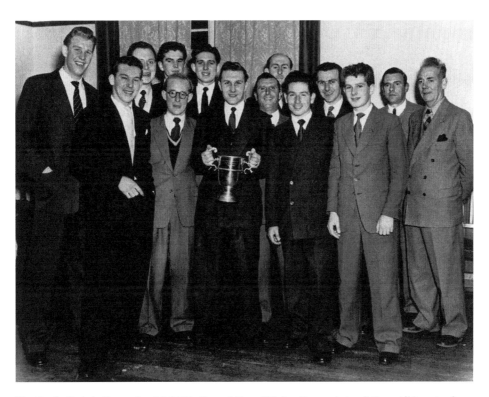

The football club dinner for 1956/7 allowed Tony White, the captain of Beer Albion, to show off the Morrison Bell Cup – probably the most prestigious cup to win in the Exeter and District League. With him are, left to right, Bob Aplin, Brian Northcott, Eddie Bond, Monty Lapin, Ron Wilkins, 'Taffy' Fowler, Jimmy Jones, Alan Westlake, Lew Perkins, Eric White, Michael Collier, White, Maurice Webber (manager) and Charlie Morris.

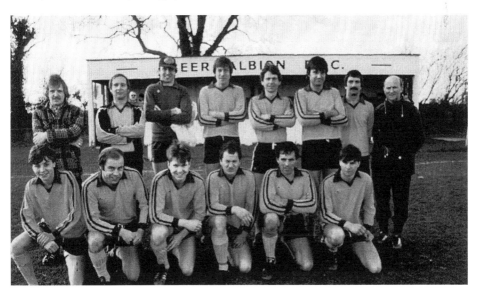

The reserve team of 1983/4.

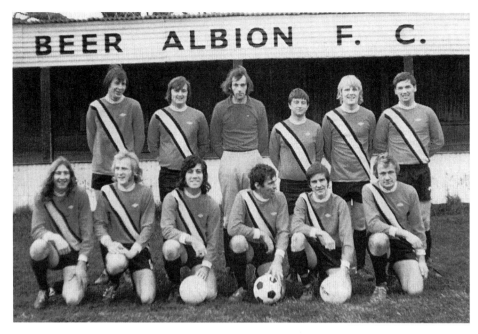

Season 1977/8 – outside the grandstand.

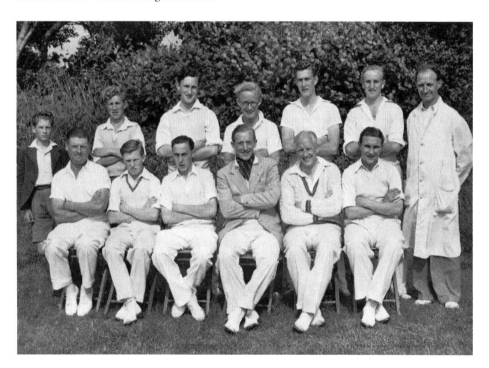

The village is not renowned for its cricket but here is a photograph of a successful side in either the 1951 or 1952 season. The team were: Eric White, Elwyn Collier, John Miller, Michael Collier, Dick Somers, John Newton, Bill Wilkins (umpire), Bill Stone, Michael Barrett, John Parish, Francis Eyles, the Revd Mr Walker, Tony White.

6

VILLAGE
CELEBRATIONS

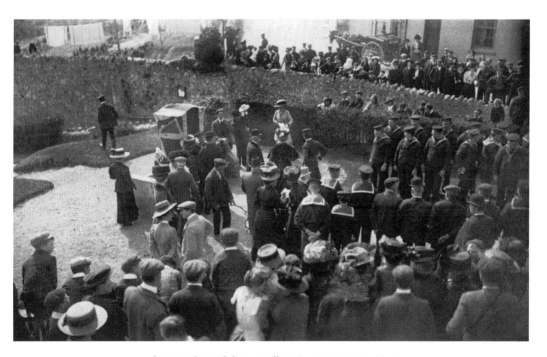

The unveiling of the Macallum Monument in 1897.

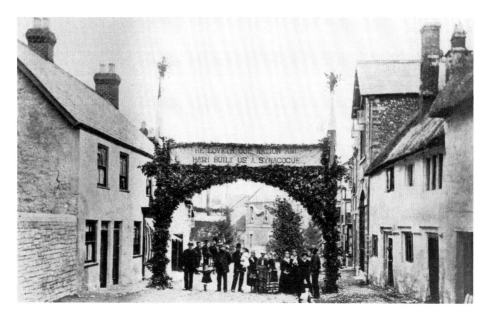

Celebrations at Beer for the opening of the new church. The opening in 1878 was long remembered by the people of the village. Luggers were drawn up in the roads with sails set, men were at their post, bands played and banners fluttered everywhere. Arches were built over the main street, inscriptions were plentiful and this one, full of fancy, went so far as to say 'HE LOVETH OUR NATION AND HATH BUILT US A SYNAGOGUE'.

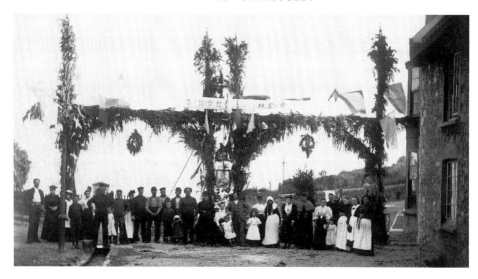

Queen Victoria's Diamond Jubilee celebrations, Beer, 1897. The possibilities of a great celebration in 1897 were first discussed after the jubilee of 1887, although it was not until 1896 that public interest in the event was thoroughly aroused. Every town and village formed a committee to arrange activities for the great day, and everywhere the streets were lavishly decorated. Pictured here are the triumphal arches that spanned Fore Street in Beer, and some of the fir trees that were dotted throughout the village. Processions, parties, sports, and many other attractions were the order of the day and the memory of this celebration stayed with people for the rest of their lives.

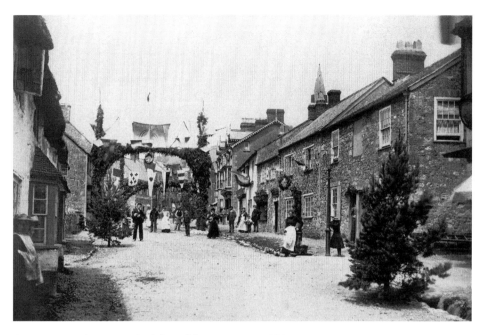

Queen Victoria's Diamond Jubilee celebrations, Beer, 1897.

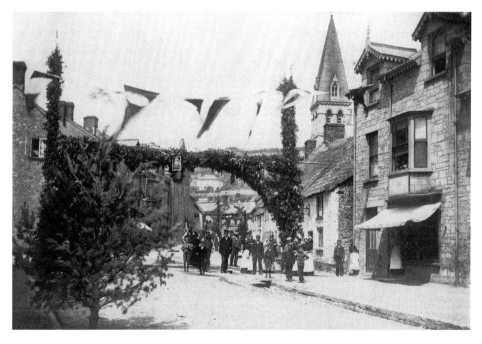

Another fine photograph of Queen Victoria's Diamond Jubilee in 1897. Note the picture of the queen in the centre of the arch and the spire of St Michael's Church, which was just nine years old.

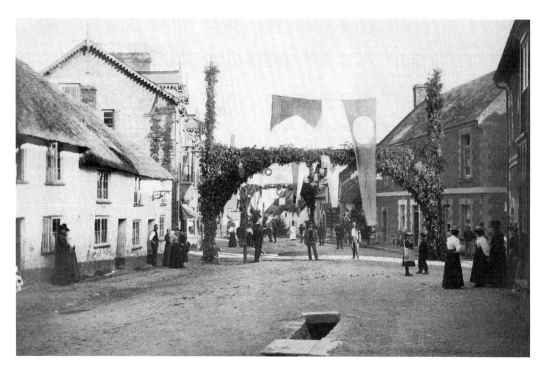

Queen Victoria's Diamond Jubilee celebrations. Standing in the doorway of their home at no. 1 Gravel Cottage are Lizzie and Bob Boles.

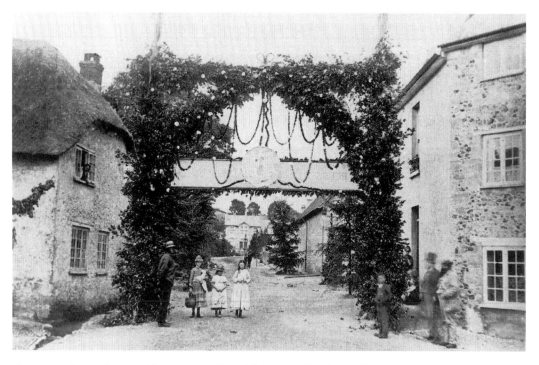

More triumphal arches to celebrate Queen Victoria's Diamond Jubilee at The Causeway.

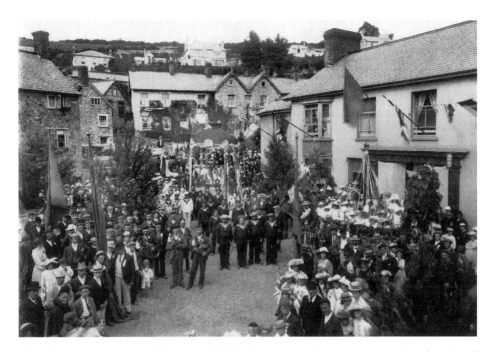

Edward VII Coronation celebrations, 1902. The coronation was an occasion of national rejoicing and a full programme for the event was arranged in Beer. The streets were lavishly decorated and at about midday there was a grand procession. The Beer Naval recruits, shown here, took part. Throughout the day the local people enjoyed themselves. King Edward was well liked and easily the most popular Prince of Wales to that date. In common with the rest of the country, the people of Beer were looking forward to a new era – the Edwardian age.

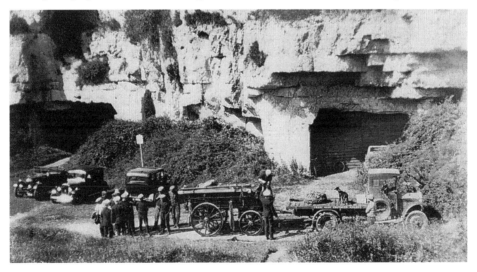

Rocket practice at Beer Quarries, September 1932. There were about four practice calls a year and these always attracted a number of spectators. In this picture we see the coastguard arriving with the wagon which held all the gear. During practice a large rocket would be fired towards the mast. A light rope was attached to the rocket, and if it successfully hit the mast, a thick hawser was then attached to the rope and hauled aboard.

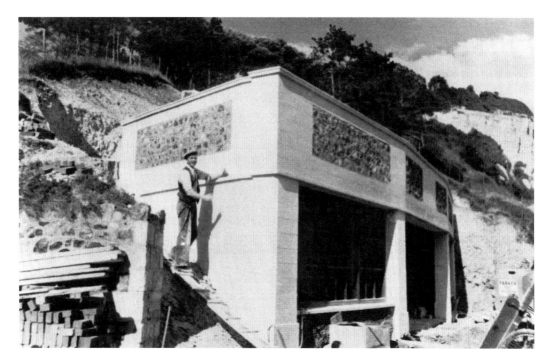

Putting the finishing touches to the shelter on the clifftop in 1954, which was given to the village in a legacy from Mr Self.

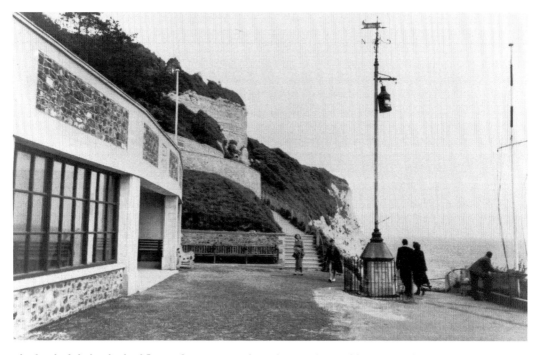

The finished shelter built of flint and Beer stone. The Fisherman's (Washbourne) Light is also illustrated well in this photograph.

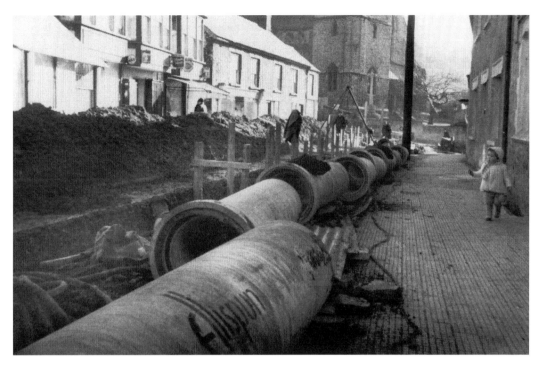

The new sewer being constructed in Fore Street in 1952.

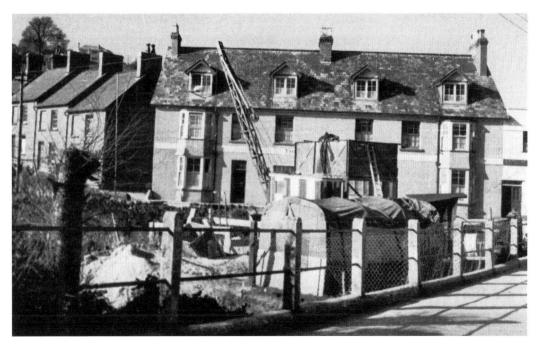

Another photograph of the works underway in the Memorial Garden opposite the Anchor Hotel. From the shaft which was sunk here, the works were tunnelled out to Beer Head and beyond into the sea. The deepest shaft was over 350ft.

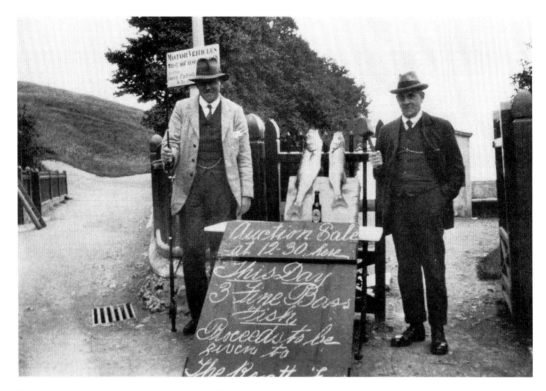

These two fine bass caught locally were sold to swell the Regatta funds of 1924.

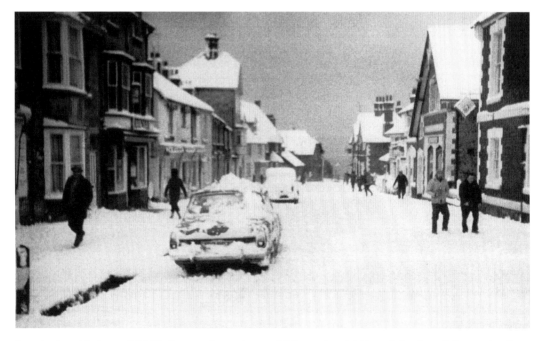

Beer in the midwinter of 1963. It started snowing on 26 December 1962 and the thaw did not take place until March the following year. This photograph dates from 5 January 1963.

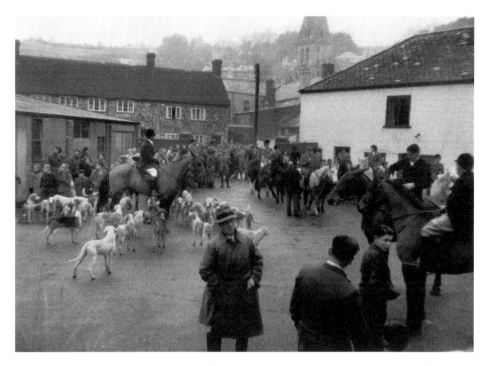

Axe Vale Hounds at the meet at the Dolphin Hotel yard on 3 January 1951. The man facing the camera was a local farmer from Rock Farm, Mr Billy Reynolds.

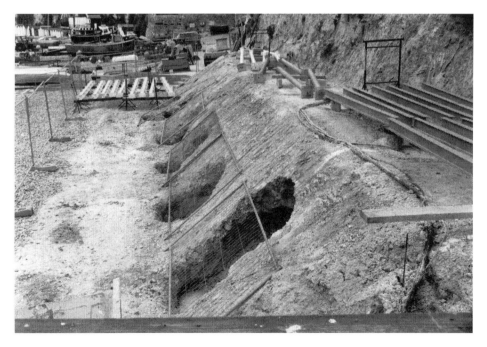

This extensive preparatory work in 1965 was to stabilise and raise the level from the beach for the top deck of beach huts.

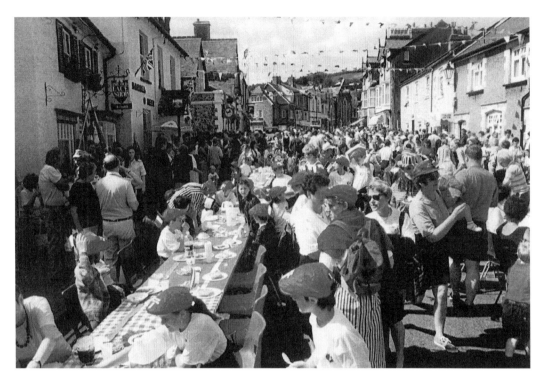

Queen Elizabeth, the Queen Mother's 100th birthday in 2000. The tables are all set up for the children's tea party.

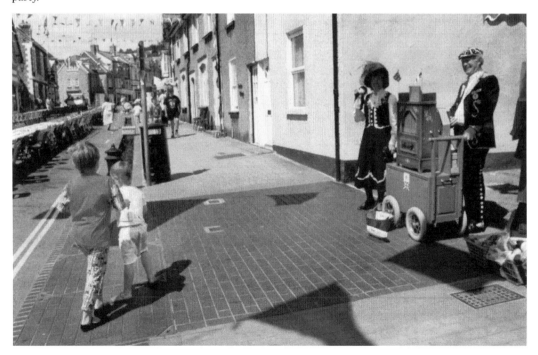

A street party at Beer for Queen Elizabeth II's Golden Jubilee in 2002.

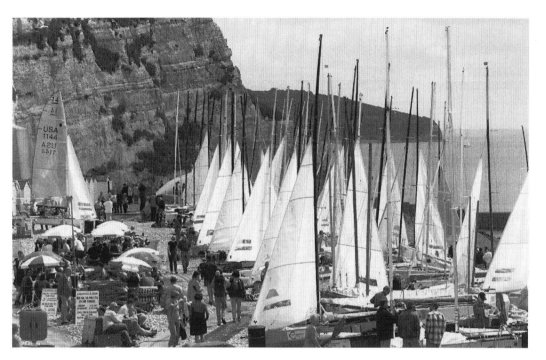

Beer Sailing Club had the honour and privilege
of hosting three major sailing competitions
with the European 14s Championship, 1993;
the Prince of Wales Cup, 1997, and in 2000 the
World 14 Championships where 115 boats from
nine nations competed. The Australian champion
came to defend his title but it was won by an
American boat. Much merriment was had during
the week of the competition and the photographs
(on this page and overleaf) show the extent of the
activity generated.

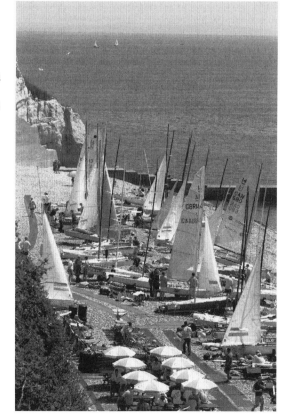

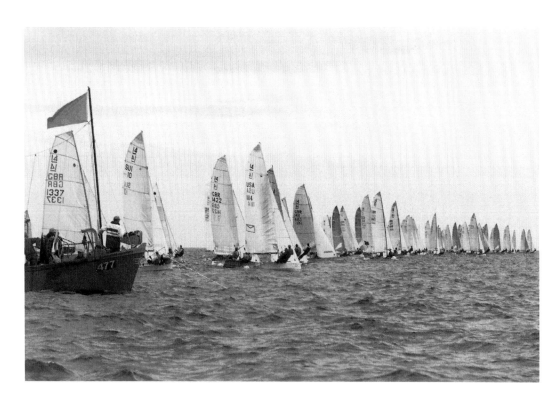

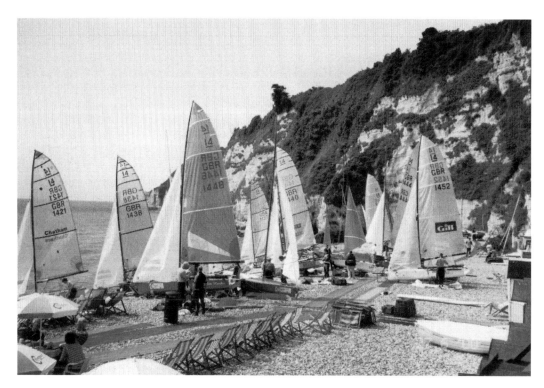

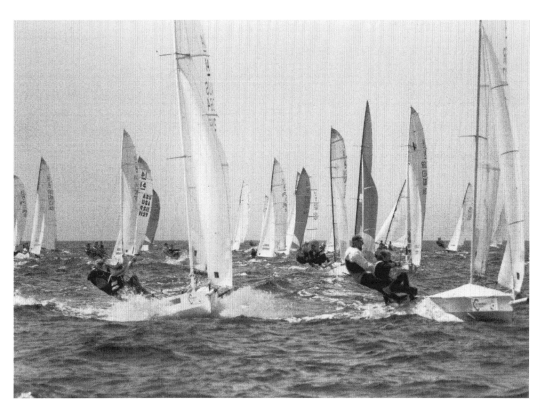

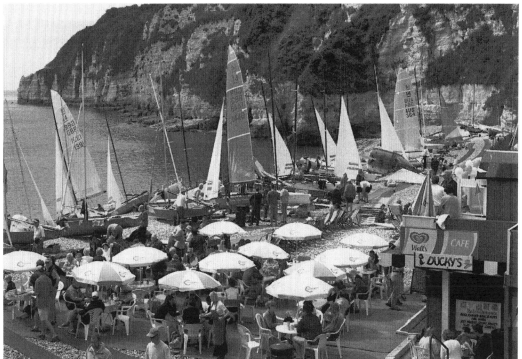

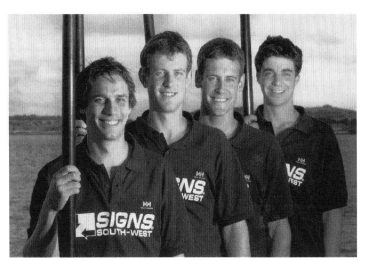

The All Relative Atlantic Rowing Team of 2005. Robert and Justin are brothers and James and Martin the brothers' first cousins. They achieved a marvellous feat in the fastest time recorded to win the race, only to lose it because they drank some water near the finish which the rules did not permit. The Beer Boys came home to a wonderful village reception and all still live here.

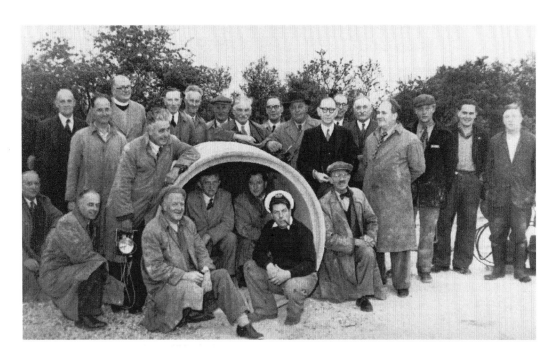

There was a complete new sewer laid from The Cross out and beyond Beer Head in 1952/3. This photograph is of Beer Parish Council and the interested parties in the project including Jack Vine (third from the right), who was the foreman for W.C. French, the contractors. After the project was completed he stayed in the village and raised his family. He died in 2010. Others in the picture include the Revd W.H. Dormer, Billy Wilkins and Jimmy Green.

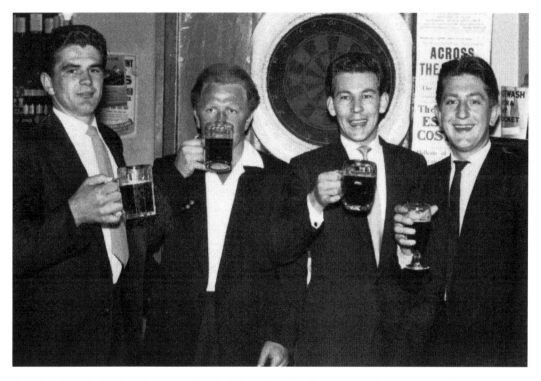

Four Beer Boys in 1957 – Monty Laptin, Ken Westlake, Brian (Juggler) Northcott and Ian White – enjoying a drink in the local.

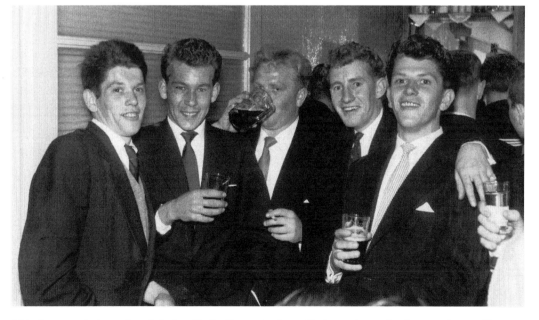

This photograph shows five of the local lads all smartly dressed before going to the dance at Seaton. They are, left to right: Stuart Barrett, Brian Northcott, Ken Westlake, Elwyn Collier and Keith Barrett.

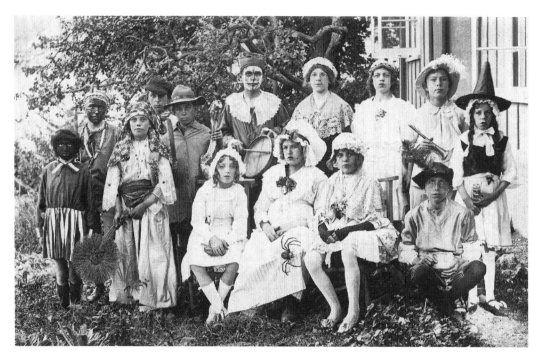

Beer folk in fancy dress in 1910, or perhaps it was a pantomime?

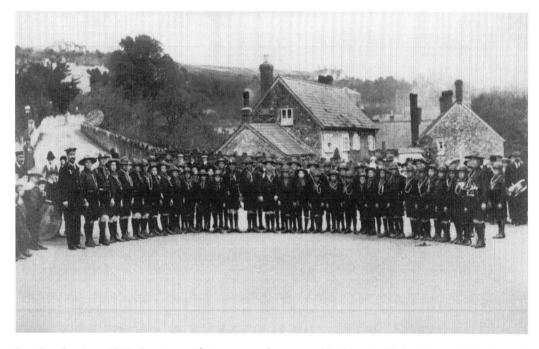

Beer Boy Scouts, *c.* 1919. Scouting with its organised games and bathing instilled self-control, fair play and manliness into boys throughout the world. The movement was received with great enthusiasm in Beer, and at the time of this photograph the troop numbered about fifty.

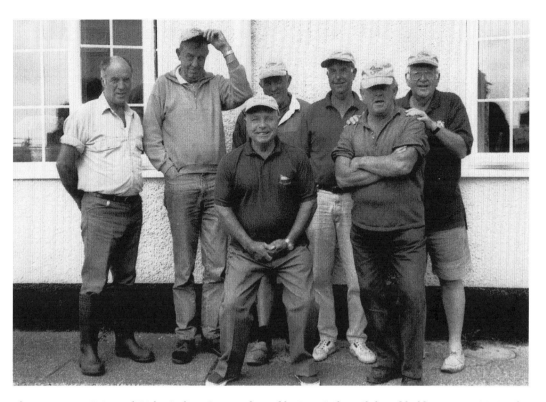

The prestigious Prince of Wales Sailing Cup was hosted by Beer Sailing Club and held in Beer in 1997. The photograph is a collection of Beer Boys gathered outside the Anchor Hotel at the completion of the event. They are Roy Newton, Bob April, Colin Westlake, Phil Bastone, Norman Lambert, Robbie Driver and Ken Westlake.

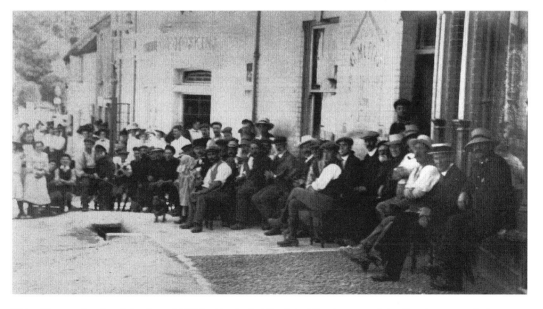

This village gathering dates from 1896 but just what the inhabitants were celebrating is unrecorded.

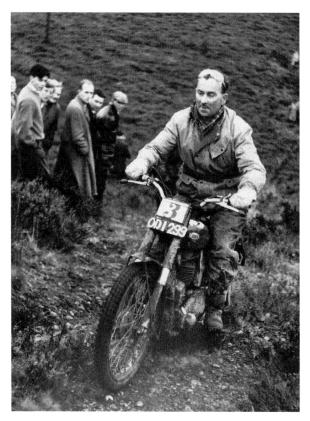

Motorcycle trials are events in which a cross-country course has to be completed within a short time, with points lost on observed sections of the course for stopping or touching the ground. With sheer determination and concentration Gerald Oborn from Beer makes his way up on observed section in a Devon trial on his BSA trials bike in about 1953.

Rethatching cottages at the bottom of Fore Street. There were no health and safety measures in the 1870s. The tall gentleman with his back to the camera is Theodore Boalch, the great-grandfather of the former owner of the Anchor Hotel which is adjacent to these former cottages.

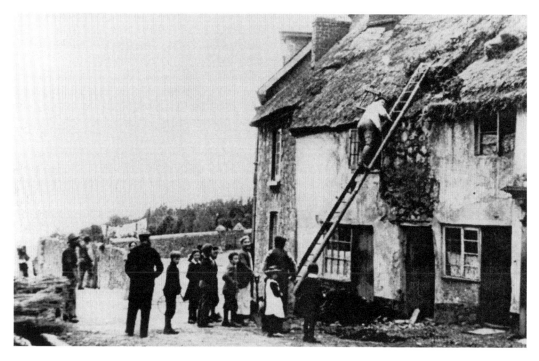

7

BEER REGATTA
& BEACH

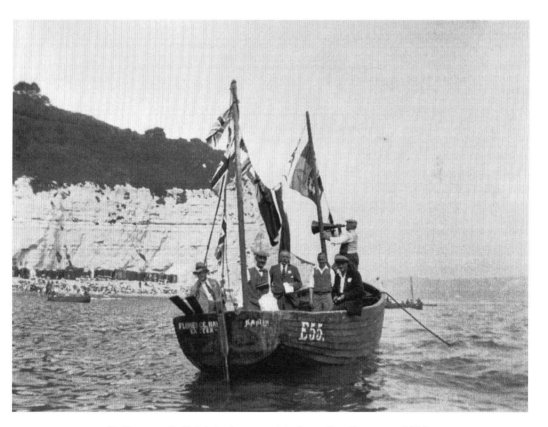

Dr Tonge and officials in the committee boat, Beer Regatta, *c.* 1935.

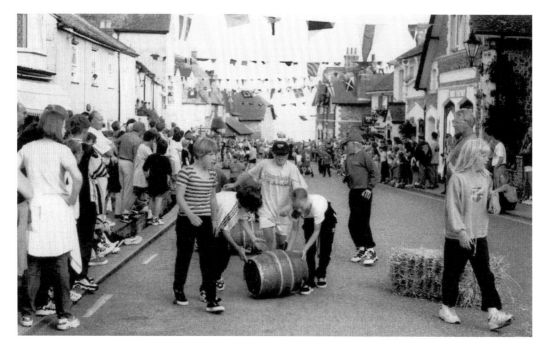

Barrel-rolling was a Tuesday night attraction to many spectators as this picture shows, but sadly it ceased when the insurance became prohibitive, resulting from health and safety requirements in 2007. No accidents had occurred and it seemed a great pity that such a popular event had to be removed from the week's programme.

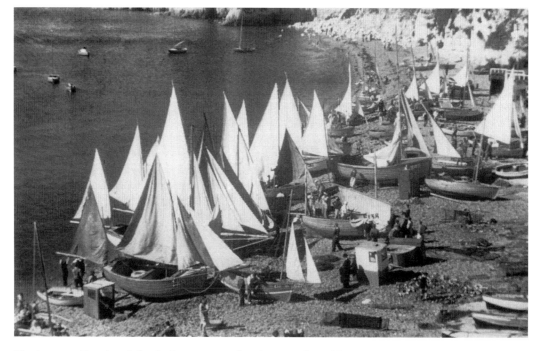

Rigging up on Beer beach for the first Regatta after the Second World War.

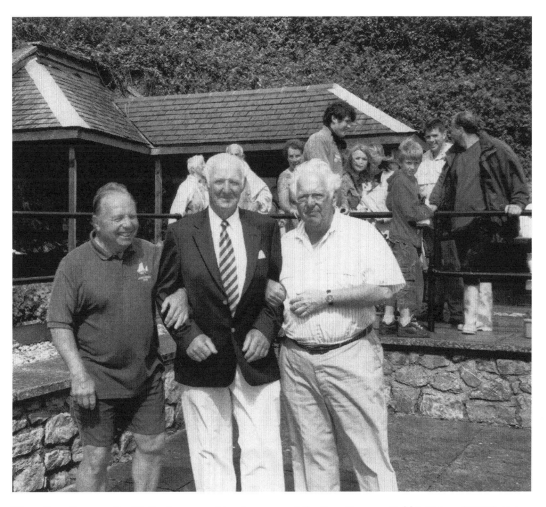

Three Beer Boys – all with the honour of having opened the Regatta – are Robbie Driver (2000), Peter Bartlett (2004) and Norman Lambert (1999).

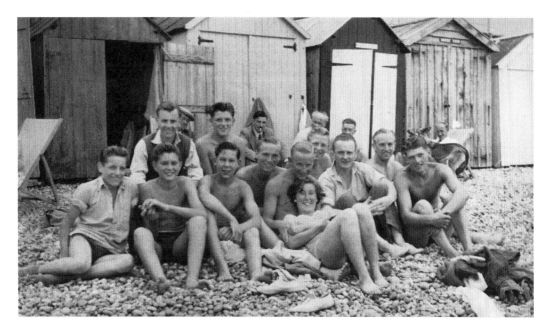

A fine gathering of Beer boys with a Beer girl – sadly six of those in this picture, taken in 1952, have passed away and the others are now senior citizens.

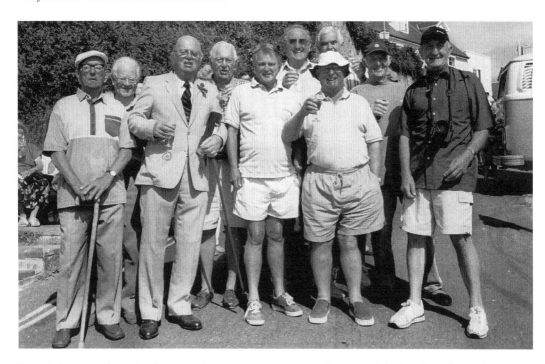

Regatta day, or week as it has become, always attracts many Beer-born people back to the village. This picture depicts a collection of Beer boys on Sea Hill for the 2003 celebrations. Among those pictured are John White, George Hookings, Alan Bricknell, Norman Lambert, Peter Harris, John Underwood, Monty Laptin (behind), Michael Collier, Peter Bartlett and Ian White.

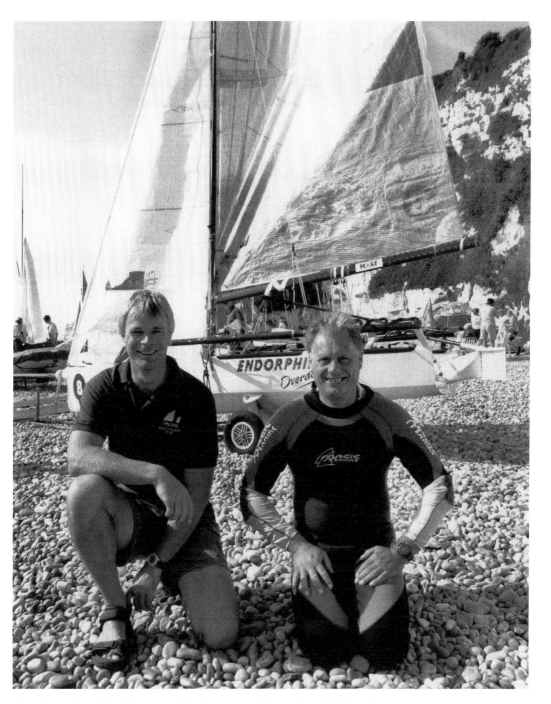

Peter Bagwell and Paul Vine, two of the Beer competitors at the 2007 Beer Regatta.

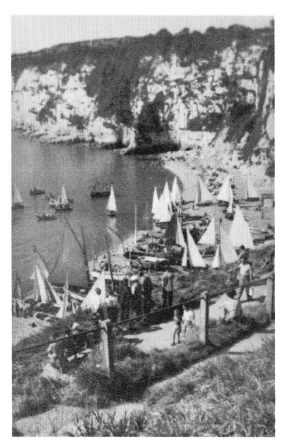

Rigging up for the 1952 Regatta at 9.45 a.m. on 14 August.

Fun on Beer beach in 1954 with four recognisable characters in Gerald Boalch, Ralph Bond, Tom Westlake and son Colin (partly hidden behind Dad).

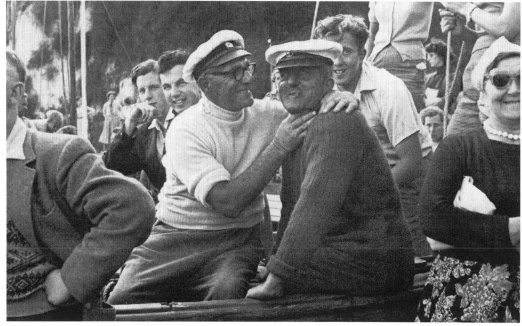

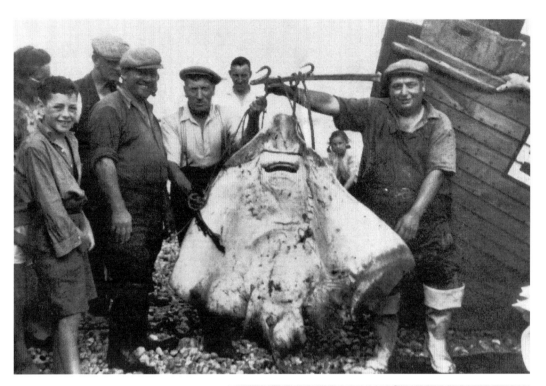

A massive skate caught by Reg Barrett and Mr Bartlett. Albert Bartlett is the man in the middle supporting the monster fish, *c.* 1947.

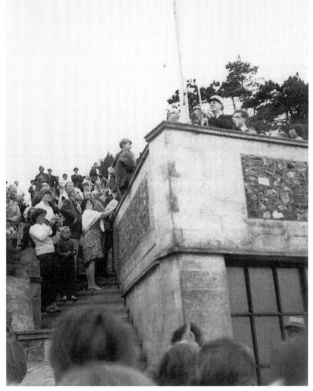

Sir Alec Rose, the round-the-world yachtsman, opening Beer Regatta in 1969.

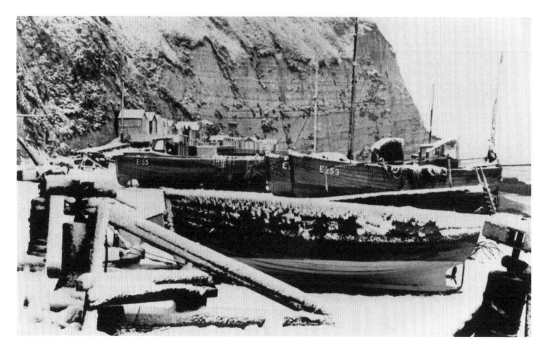

One of the heaviest falls of snow took place immediately following the festive season of 1962/3. Rarely does Beer beach retain snow to the degree shown here.

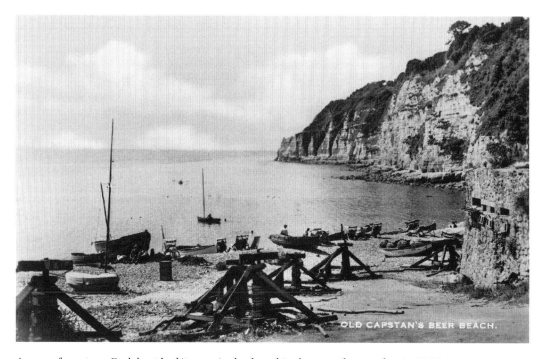

A mass of capstans. Each boat had its own in the days this photograph was taken in 1946.

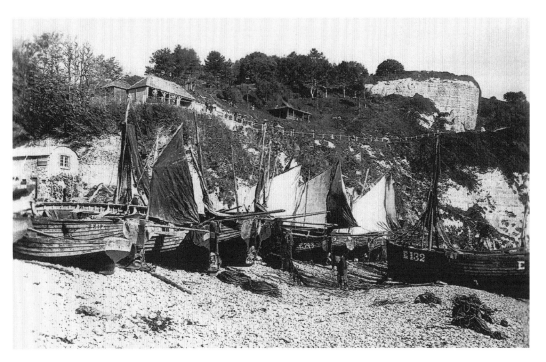

This picture was taken by Mr Morton (an author and journalist) in 1927. He visited Beer each year and here captures the village industry of fishing extremely well.

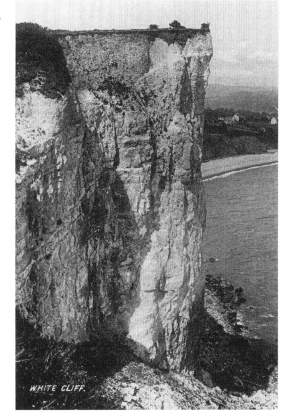

White Cliff rises some 390ft above sea level at low tide and is equidistant between Beer and Seaton boundary, which is approached from either the cliff path or coastal walk. Seaton beach is on the right of the picture.

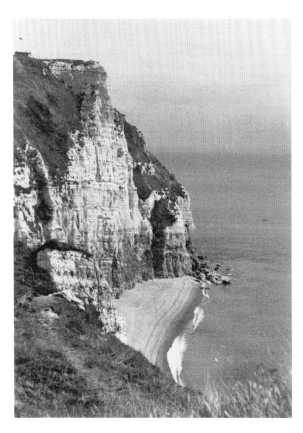

Beer Head with the coastguard hut and flat on the headland and Poundswell Beach below, 1948.

In about 1905 three fishermen go down over Sea Hill – note the group up the street and the three people outside the Bay Tea Rooms.

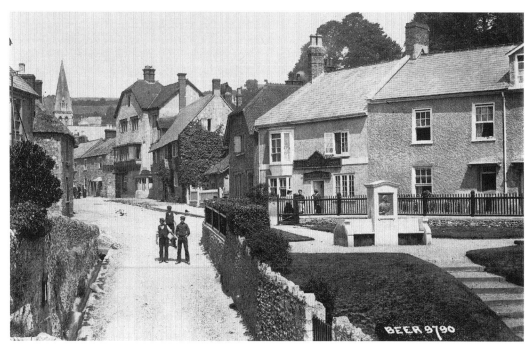

The reigning World 14s Australian sailors defending their title at Beer in 2000. They lost it to the Americans.

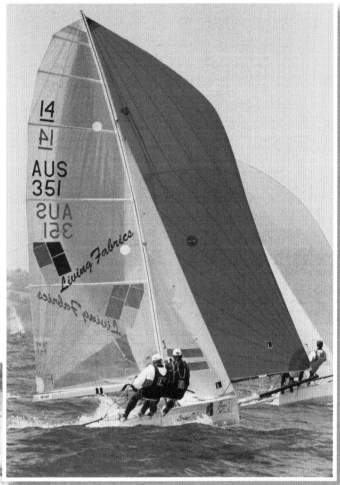

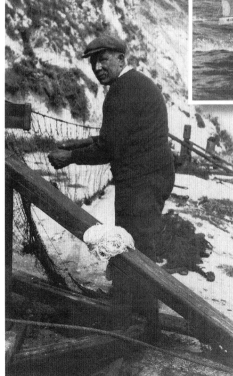

Clifford or William Chapple, *c.* 1930.

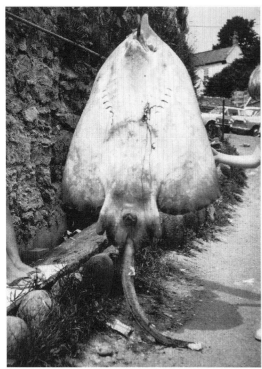

A photograph of the locally caught skate whose weight exceeded 100lb. Some fish!

Devastation on Beer beach following a storm in the 1970s.

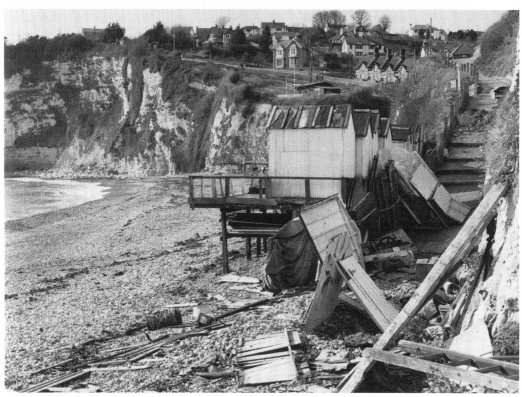

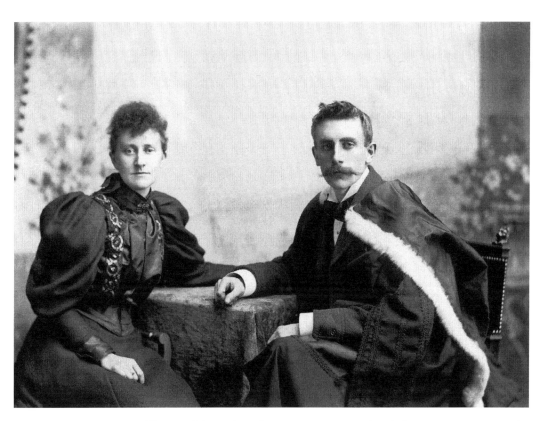

Dr Edward Tonge is pictured here with his wife in about 1900. A native of Yorkshire, Dr Tonge came to the Beer practice in 1897 where he remained until his death in 1937. He took a keen and practical interest in the affairs of the village, giving help and encouragement wherever needed, never sparing himself in the cause of others. He lived for his work and faithful to his self-imposed duty, he left his own sickbed to minister to those whose needs were greater. The great care that he gave to the people of Beer endeared him to everyone. His name became synonymous with Beer and when he died aged sixty-four, the entire community mourned him. During the First World War he was Principal Medical Officer in charge of the Seaton Auxiliary Hospital sited at Ryalls Court. He also acted as an Admiralty Surgeon. For that work Dr Tonge was awarded the OBE. Although the Gosling family lived at Seaton, Dr Tonge was their family doctor, and in 1929 he brought young Ted Gosling into the world. His parents named him Edward, after Dr Tonge.

ACKNOWLEDGMENTS

L ike the first step on the moon, photography brought a giant leap forward for men, recording history in all its forms as well as much else. Preservation is essential and one wonders just how many local photographs would have survived and been available to the general public in a book such as this if it were not for people like Norman Lambert, who with his interest, determination, application and hard work has built up a wonderful collection of old photographs and postcards depicting people and events – the stuff of local history.

With Norman I would like to thank all those who have spoken from their own personal knowledge of times past and a lifetime's interest in the village of Beer.

We are most grateful to Sally Stratton for her assistance with the compilation of the book and we would also like to thank Michelle Tilling at The History Press for her much appreciated help.

Old photographs and postcards are truly fascinating. They bring back times past with intensity and to live in them is to never die.

Ted Gosling